Sammy and Rosie Get Laid
The Script and the Diary

HANIF KUREISHI

faber and faber

LONDON · BOSTON

First published in 1988
by Faber and Faber Limited
3 Queen Square London WC1N 3AU

Photoset by Parker Typesetting Service Leicester
Printed in Great Britain by
Richard Clay Ltd, Bungay, Suffolk
All rights reserved

British Library Cataloguing in Publication Data

Kureishi, Hanif
Sammy and Rosie get laid and some time with Stephen.
I. Title
822'.914   PR6061.U
ISBN 0-571-15000-4

For My Parents

Sammy and Rosie Get Laid opened in London on 15 January 1988.
The cast included:

RAFI	Shashi Kapoor
ALICE	Claire Bloom
SAMMY	Ayub Khan Din
ROSIE	Frances Barber
DANNY	Roland Gift
ANNA	Wendy Gazelle
VIVIA	Suzette Llewellyn
RANI	Meera Syal
CABBIE/GHOST	Badl Uzzaman

Producers	Tim Bevan and Sarah Radclyffe
Director	Stephen Frears
Screenplay	Hanif Kureishi
Lighting cameraman	Oliver Stapleton
Production designer	Hugo Luczyc Wyhowski
Editor	Mick Audsley
Music	Stanley Myers

Contents

Sammy and Rosie Get Laid

1. INT. TUBE STATION. DAY

A young black man, DANNY, stands in the open doors of a tube train. The doors are shutting. He holds them apart for an old woman to get through, yells up at the train guard, slips out himself, and runs up the platform. The tube platform is filled with music from a large straggly band of kids who play in a tunnel off the platform.

2. EXT. STREET. DAY

A South London street. It is a residential area, foul, rundown. The police are tying off the street with white tape. A number of people have gathered to look on – some to protest. A mixture of black and white. But people are taken by surprise. Outside a house in the street are two police vans. The police are running about. The police are armed.

3. EXT. YARD. DAY

The yard of a poor house in the South London street. A high wall surrounds the yard. A dog runs round and round the yard, barking, chasing its tail. We hold on this wretched dog for as long as possible or bearable – maybe intercutting it with incidents from scene 2.

4. INT. KITCHEN. DAY

The kitchen looks out on the yard. A middle-aged black woman is cooking in the kitchen. A frying pan full of bacon and tomatoes. Also a full chip pan bubbling away. The woman talks and laughs with her son, a young black man sitting at the kitchen table playing the trumpet.

5. EXT. YARD. DAY

And now the police, armed, jump over the wall into the yard. The dog goes berserk.
Cut to: Now the police are breaking into the front of the house.
Cut to: At the tied-off section of the street we see DANNY. He presses against the tape, looking anxiously towards the house.
Cut to: In the kitchen, the kid sees the police coming over the wall. He stands up and sits down. Then runs to the door of the kitchen. This door leads to a hall.
Cut to: DANNY, at the tape, takes out a pair of scissors or a knife and cuts through the tape. People surge forward now, past the police.

Cut to: The woman's hall is full of police. They are trying to grab the boy. The woman runs screaming into the hall. She carries the chip pan. She hurls it at the police, spraying them with boiling fat. A young hysterical cop at the end of the hall, frightened and confused, blasts two bullets into the woman's body. She falls to the ground.
Cut to: Outside, DANNY *has got to the house now. He hears the shots. There is chaos.*

TITLES

6. INT. ANNA'S STUDIO. DAY
We see a woman's naked back. She has a 'W' tattooed on each buttock. Behind it the sound of a man and woman in bed together. The woman is on top of the man. They are not copulating but playing. Numerous official papers are spread everywhere. SAMMY *then tries to write something down but* ANNA *bites him. She is American.* SAMMY, *in his late twenties, wears an open black shirt. We are in Anna's photographic studio. It is a huge room, in a converted warehouse, rather like a New York loft. Video and photographic equipment. Also many Indian things: fabrics, carvings, carpets, pictures of plump gurus, etc. On the table next to them is a cat. Through the open window trees are visible and the sound of kids playing is heard. A dog barks in the distance. The sound of an aeroplane.*

7. INT. AEROPLANE. DAY
Cross-fade on to each buttock of the swaying arse two seats in the plane. One seat is empty. In the other sits RAFI, *a suave old man with an angelic face. He is always exquisitely dressed in English suits.* RAFI *takes a large sherbet out of a paper bag and pops it into his mouth, sucking contentedly, with white sherbet on the end of his nose. The captain addresses the aircraft: 'We are approaching London, Heathrow, and will be landing shortly . . . the temperature in London is . . .'*

8. INT. ANNA'S STUDIO. DAY
SAMMY *and* ANNA *are in bed.* ANNA *laughs as* SAMMY *tries to get up, against her wishes.*
SAMMY: As your accountant, Anna, I think we should look for some offshore investments for you. (*Pause.*) Now I've gotta

2

go, baby. Meet someone at the airport.

ANNA: You'll get pimples on your tongue for telling lies, you couch potato. You mean your wife's got the dinner on and you gotta get home.

SAMMY: My wife. It's funny, Anna, the more Rosie hears about you, the more she's knocked out by you.

ANNA: (*Pulling his outstretched tongue*) That's another one – right there.

SAMMY: She's especially intrigued and totally knocked out by you having a 'W' tattooed on each buttock. Rosie wants to know if it's some kind of New York code.

ANNA: You know what it is, you couch potato. It's just so that if I bend over it spells 'wow'!

9. INT. COUNCIL FLAT. DAY

ROSIE, *beautiful and well dressed, about thirty, a social worker, walks through an old man's filthy falling-down council flat. There are many photographs of his children and grandchildren.* ROSIE *looks for him.*

ROSIE: Mr Weaver, Mr Weaver! It's Rosie Hobbs!
(*She sits down in the middle of the room for a moment and we hold on her face. We hear* SAMMY'*s voice.*)

SAMMY: (*Voice over*) There's two things my main squeeze Rosie doesn't believe in. Getting the dinner on and sexual fidelity. She says jealousy is wickeder than adultery.
(*Cut to: now* ROSIE *pushes open the door of the old man's bathroom.*)
(*Voice over*) Rosie doesn't want to possess anyone. If she could see us now doing your accounts she'd feel so unpossessive she'd open a bottle of champagne.

10. EXT. HEATHROW AIRPORT. DAY
Surrounded by suitcases RAFI *stands, waiting for his son* SAMMY *outside the airport terminal. He is getting very impatient. Finally he waves at the nearest cab and picks up his suitcases.*

11. INT. ANNA'S STUDIO. DAY
SAMMY *lies there, greedily cracking another beer. Meanwhile* ANNA *has got up and is adjusting photographic screens around the bed.*

3

SAMMY: I haven't seen my old man for five years. When he was young and poor he lived in England. Then he went home to get powerful. He dumped me with my mother when they split up. He never wanted me. He left me here. I think I must have been the result of a premature ejaculation.

12. EXT. AIRPORT. DAY

We see RAFI *getting into the cab. The cab drives away. The* CABBIE *is an Asian man in a brown suit. One eye is bandaged and part of his skull has been smashed in.* RAFI *doesn't notice this but it's important we see and remember the* CABBIE's *face.*

SAMMY: (*Voice over*) Rosie and I visited him there. He's a great patriarch and a little king, surrounded by servants.

(*Cut to: In the studio* ANNA *is ready to photograph* SAMMY.)

ANNA: You worship him, don't you? Does he have any kids from his other wife?

SAMMY: Not really. Only daughters.

(*They laugh.*)

Give me a comb, will ya, Anna?

13. INT. COUNCIL FLAT. DAY

SAMMY: (*Voice over*) Anna, he's got to see me at my best tonight – plenty of dough, decent flat, Rosie not looking too tired.

(ROSIE *has pushed the bathroom door. She goes into the bathroom. The walls are peeling. Water drips from the walls. The old man is dead in the bath, his thin body under the water. His head is jaundice yellow. The water steams. She stares at him and pulls out the plug, accidentally touching his leg.*)

14. INT./EXT. CAB. DAY

It is dusk now. RAFI *in the cab is well into London, heading towards the grimmer stretches of South London.*

RAFI: (*To* CABBIE) For me England is hot buttered toast on a fork in front of an open fire. And cunty fingers.

(*The cab stops in the traffic.* RAFI *pulls down the window and sticks his old grey head out. The cab accelerates. Above* RAFI, *and around him, he sees criss-crossed motorways, flyovers, huge direction indicators, and a swirl of fast-moving traffic, dreamlike, noisy, strange. We see it through his eyes as if for the first time. This isn't the England he remembers.*)

15. EXT. BALCONY OF TOWER BLOCK. DAY

ROSIE *stands on the balcony of the tower block where the old man lives. It is on one of those estates that look as if they have been transplanted from the outskirts of Warsaw. She is waiting for the ambulance. She looks out over London, towards the concrete sledge of the motorway in the distance. Then she looks down. A group of youngish kids knock on the door of the flat opposite. They push the owner aside and steam into the flat, wearing masks and scarves tied around their faces. Down on the ground, in the centre of the courtyard, there is a huge bonfire burning. Black and white kids stoke it, throwing things on. The ambulance, its siren going, lights flashing, screams into the courtyard.*

16. INT. SAMMY'S AND ROSIE'S BATHROOM. DAY

ROSIE *is now washing her hair in their 'Victorian' bathroom. She plunges her hair into the water. She pulls her head out. We hold on her face and see her hair full of water. This could be shot, perhaps using a mirror, so that we can see through into the large, long, living room. There are several of* ROSIE's *women friends gathered here, plus one white and one black boy, both deaf and dumb, who dance to music. Then one of the women,* RANI, *appears behind* ROSIE, *banging the door shut.*

RANI: Rosie, there's trouble outside. I think there will be fires tonight.
>(ROSIE *turns and looks at her. Then they look into the bathroom mirror. They do not see themselves but instead a derelict shed in a green wood. It is pouring with rain. In the shed a young man is painting a portrait of* ROSIE.)

ROSIE: That's my lover, Walter. I'm seeing him later.

RANI: What will Sammy say about that?

ROSIE: Though a forest fire will have broken out in his heart, lungs and liver, his tongue will try to say: What an interesting life you have, Rosie.

RANI: How damaging for him.

17. EXT. STREETS. DUSK

Now RAFI's *cab enters the South London street where* SAMMY *and*

ROSIE *live*.

RAFI: (*To* CABBIE) My son Sammy is a very successful accountant.

CABBIE: And he lives here?

(*Halfway up, the street is blocked by police cars, police vans, and an ambulance. This is the street from scene 2. The cab stops. It cannot go any further. We see puzzled* RAFI *taking in the chaotic scene. Now* RAFI, *with his suitcases, walks past the police cars and ambulance. The exteriors at night have a heightened, unreal feel. As* RAFI *passes by the terraced house from scene 3, two ambulance men carry out a body on a stretcher. A crowd of black people and some whites have gathered outside, many truculent, others weeping.* DANNY *stands apart from it all. His young black girlfriend and their kid are there now, with him.* RAFI *walks past, taking it all in. We hold fully and carefully on the faces.* RAFI *walks past some larger houses. The* CABBIE *watches him. On the steps of these houses* ROSIE *and* VIVIA *are standing, anxiously watching the ambulance incident.* RAFI *pushes his way through the crowd,* DANNY *watching him.* ROSIE *spots* RAFI *in the crowd and rushes down into the midst of it all to get him, pushing her way through.*)

ROSIE: Rafi! Rafi!

(*She finds him and embraces him.* DANNY *is watching.*)

What's wrong? Didn't Sammy pick you up?

RAFI: The only thing that boy's picking up at the moment is a sexually transmitted disease!

18. INT. SAMMY'S AND ROSIE'S FLAT. EVENING

A spacious flat, plenty of books stacked up, a jungle of plants, some decent prints, music playing. The flat is wild and untidy, not yuppie. Charts and maps on the walls, pictures of flowers, old Buddhas, lots of junk furniture, home-made sculpture, bidets full of books, velvet curtains on the walls, huge wrecked armchairs, layers of Turkish carpets, hookahs, brass pots, high-tech accoutrements . . . a hammock strung across the window, red silk billowing down from the ceiling. Four of Rosie's friends are drinking wine: EVA, RANI, BRIDGET *and* MARGY. EVA *is a Jewish intellectual.* BRIDGET *has her head shaved at the sides, the rest of her hair is long.* MARGY *is very committed politically.* BRIDGET *and* EVA *massage each other.*

MARGY: (*Ironic*) Sammy may be an accountant, but he's a radical accountant . . .

RANI: (*To* BRIDGET) Won't you massage me? Don't I need support too? Where's Rosie and Vivia gone?

BRIDGET: (*Part of a continuing conversation*) I've always been on the pill. Better cancer than pregnant. I've never even seen a rubber. I'm not that generation. Margy?
(*Meanwhile the white boy is rubbing himself off on the carpet.* RANI *pulls him up and he stares panting at the women. They ignore him.*)

MARGY: I always carry half a dozen with me. In case I meet a tall dark, hard stranger.
(*She pulls a packet of rubbers out of her pocket.*)

19. INT. STAIRS. EVENING

ROSIE *and* VIVIA *struggle up the stairs with Rafi's suitcases. This area of the flats is also spacious and open.* RAFI *climbs up the broad stone steps in front of them, with immaculate dignity as usual.*

RAFI: Is this world war typical of your streets?

ROSIE: (*To* RAFI) The police shot a woman by mistake. They were looking for her son. It's easy enough to mistake a fifty-year-old office cleaner for a twenty-year-old jazz trumpeter.
(*When* RAFI *and* VIVIA *come into the room they see and hear:*)

MARGY: You hold the condom there and pull down.
(*MARGY pulls the condom down over a large knobbly carrot. The women have gathered round to look and laugh.*)

EVA: Carrots are certainly more attractive than ding-dongs. And more prolific in vitamins, I'd imagine.
(*Now* RAFI *stands there slightly bewildered. He also sees the deaf and dumb boys, one of whom tries to dance with him.* RANI *watches* RAFI *carefully. She recognizes him.*)

ROSIE: Rafi, these are my friends.

RAFI: (*Under his breath*) Good God, are they really?
(*MARGY is hastily rolling the condom off the carrot.*)

BRIDGET: (*To* VIVIA) Everything all right outside?

VIVIA: Not at all. Let's go, Margy. Eva. Everyone.
(*MARGY bites into the carrot. They get up.* ROSIE *takes* RAFI's *arm and leads him away from the women to show him the flat.* VIVIA, *who is in the early stages of seducing* RANI, *looks*

7

expectantly at her.)

RANI: (*To* VIVIA) I'll see you later. I'll stay for a while.

VIVIA: Will you ring me?

RANI: Yes, yes.

(*They take each other's hands and kiss goodbye, a longish tonguey kiss, which* RAFI *sees and is rather thrown by.* RANI *looks up defiantly at him.* VIVIA, *laughing at this, leads the women out.* RANI *joins* ROSIE, *who is showing* RAFI *the flat. The deaf and dumb boys peer through the foliage at* RAFI.)

ROSIE: How d'you like our place, Rafi?

RANI: Aren't they just in clover?

RAFI: Well, 50 per cent clover, 50 per cent synthetic materials.

RANI: Have you entirely retired from politics, Mr Rahman?

RAFI: Oh yes, yes.

RANI: Asians in Britain have followed your political career with absolute fascination. I'd love to interview you for a paper I'm involved with.

(RAFI *shakes his head and puts his arms around* ROSIE.)

RAFI: I'm here as a purely private person.

RANI: Mr Rahman, someone like you could never be a purely private person.

20. INT. FRONT DOOR OF FLAT. EVENING

ROSIE *is saying goodbye to* RANI *and kissing her.* RAFI, *not seen by them, is walking towards the kitchen. When he hears* RANI *and* ROSIE *talking about him he stops in a place where he can overhear them.* RANI *has the deaf and dumb boys with her.*

ROSIE: Why are you so interested in Rafi?

RANI: How much d'you know about him?

ROSIE: Only that he was something in the government over there. He's always claiming to be a friend of Mao Tse-tung.

RANI: Not that that'll get him into any nightclubs. I'll dig out some stuff about him. I think it'll interest you.

21. INT. LIVING ROOM. EVENING

RAFI *sits at the table. Everyone has gone now.* RAFI *steadily eats his main course, having finished the avocado.* ROSIE *shouts through to him.*

ROSIE: I expect Sammy's got stuck with a client. He's got a lot of freelance work – actors, disc jockeys, photographers. The cream of the scum use Sammy.

22. EXT. MOTORWAY. DUSK

We are on the motorway through London. A high shot of sunset over London town. We close in to see SAMMY *in his car, shirt open to the waist, driving frantically at high speed, loud music playing in the car. A straggly band of kids, about twelve or fifteen of them, strangely dressed, some carrying musical instruments, have just crossed the motorway. Now they are climbing the rim of it and down, throwing a long rope over the side. One plays the trumpet, another a drum, one more the violin, etc. They are white and black, men and women.*

RAFI: (*Voice over*) My boy is very well respected?

ROSIE: (*Voice over*) For an accountant.

23. INT. LIVING ROOM. EVENING

Now ROSIE *is sitting down for her food. She takes a long gulp of wine.* RAFI *watches her censoriously.*

RAFI: (*Eating*) I hear the food in the West is a tribute to chemistry rather than nature.

ROSIE: (*Drinking quickly*) What do you want to do in London, Rafi?

RAFI: I want to see you both, because I love you. Plus there's an old friend I have here, Alice. And before I die I must know my beloved London again: for me it is the centre of civilization – tolerant, intelligent and completely out of control now, I hear.

ROSIE: That depends on which newspaper you read.

24. EXT. STREET. EVENING

Having necessarily dumped his car nearby, SAMMY *is running along the street towards the house. But he can't get through the crowd. The ambulance has gone. There are several police vans instead. Black and white kids have gathered in the street. The atmosphere is very heavy.* DANNY *stands there. A white kid of about thirteen on a bicycle rides after* SAMMY.

KID: Hey, dude. Dude. Wanna buy some black hash? Coke?

    (SAMMY *is now with the* KID. *As the* KID *sells him some stuff:*)

SAMMY: What the fuck's going on here, man?

9

KID: Shooting. Bad murder, man. Big trouble.

25. INT. SAMMY'S AND ROSIE'S LIVING ROOM. EVENING
ROSIE *and* RAFI *talk at the table.*

RAFI: There has been a strong hand on this country, yes?

ROSIE: The working class have not been completely beaten down
by it but –

RAFI: Exactly. In my country the English not-working class we
call them. In my factory people really work. That is how
wealth is created.
(*He helps himself to food. She grinds pepper over it.*)
Luckily black is my favourite colour.

ROSIE: Rafi, you are still wicked.

RAFI: And you are still my favourite daughter-in-law. Look. To
prove it I'll give you something. (*Pulls a rather wretched cap
out of a brown bag.*) Put it on!
(*She puts it on.*)
Who do you think gave it to me! Mao Tse-tung, that's who!
(*A sound behind them. Through the foliage they turn to see*
SAMMY *at the door, looking exhausted, terrible.*)

SAMMY: Hallo, Dad. Rosie. Sorry I'm late. I was just looking into
one or two important avenues. (*To* ROSIE) What have you got
on your head?

ROSIE: The Chinese revolution.
(*Cut to: The meal is over and* ROSIE *and* SAMMY *are now
clearing the table.* SAMMY *has a beer in each hand, sandwich in
gob.*)

RAFI: Of course Auntie Rani's dog bites everyone, including her
husband, the children –

ROSIE: (*Coldly*) I'm going out soon, Samir.

RAFI: – and the servants . . .

SAMMY: (*To* ROSIE) Where? Tonight? Tonight?

RAFI: But she won't have the dog destroyed. I'd put a bullet
through his balls myself. Wouldn't you, Sammy?

SAMMY: (*To* ROSIE) Don't go anywhere tonight. Something's
happening out there. It'll be bloody, you know.

ROSIE: When black people were attacked before and defended
themselves, you didn't used to stay in and have your supper.

SAMMY: My father's here, Rosie.

ROSIE: One of my cases died today. An old man. You wonder
what your own life means. I hate my job, picking up the
smashed pieces of people's lives. Everyone despises you for
it: the people whose lives you're poking into, and the others
who think you're pretending to be a fucking saint.
(RAFI *watches them. He gets up.*)
RAFI: I will recover. Am I in your own room?
SAMMY: (*Perfunctory*) We're putting you in Rosie's study.
(RAFI *goes.*)
ROSIE: Don't hurt him.
SAMMY: He did abandon me years ago. He's a stranger to me.
ROSIE: I think he wants to know you again.

26. INT. ROSIE'S STUDY. EVENING
*A huge dark wood desk. A large framed photo of Virginia Woolf and
a photograph of Rodin's* The Kiss. *Many books. A bed has been
installed for* RAFI. *He unpacks his numerous medicines: ointments,
pills, suppositories.*
SAMMY: (*Voice over*) Stay with us tonight, Rosie.
ROSIE: (*Voice over*) I've arranged to see Walter.
(*Cut back to living room.*)
SAMMY: Your boyfriend. Lover.
ROSIE: I said I would. But I am honest with you at least. (*Pause.*)
Sammy. Freedom plus commitment. Those were our words.
They were to be the two pillars of our love and life together.
(*Cut back to the study:* RAFI *unwraps a suppository. As he does
so he pulls aside the curtain and looks out of the window. He sees
aggressive people running about. And in the distance a car burns
– the flames strangely shooting straight up in the air. Nearer, a
group of kids, black and white, some of them masked, are kicking
down a wall, gathering the bricks up and running off with them.*)
(*Voice over*) Didn't we agree? I'll tell you what I want. I don't
want deadness or order. (*Cut to living room.*)
(*Putting her coat on*) Sometimes I want a little passion.
SAMMY: Don't let me stand in your way.
ROSIE: (*Kindly*) I can't always mother you, baby.

27. EXT. STREET. EVENING
ROSIE *runs up the street past the kids kicking the wall down. She runs*

towards the burning car. Firemen are now trying to reach it, but the kids, joyfully, are succeeding in keeping them back. One kid has a ghetto-blaster with him. ANNA *is there photographing everything, posing people by the car.* ROSIE *watches her, laughing at her charming cheek.*

28. INT. ROSIE'S STUDY. EVENING

SAMMY *tucks* RAFI *up in bed. He pulls the curtains on the wild street.*
SAMMY: We thought we'd give you a room with a view. And
    here's some cotton-wool for your earholes.
    (*Outside someone screams and there's an explosion.*
    A petrol bomb.)
    I expect it's a wild street party.
RAFI: Where's Rosie?
SAMMY: Just popped out for some fresh air.
RAFI: How's married life? Good? Bad?
SAMMY: Married life? It's a scream.
RAFI: (*Taking* SAMMY'*s hand*) Son, I am in great danger. I am
    here in London partly because my life is threatened there.
SAMMY: Who from? (*Pause.*) Can't you tell me?
RAFI: Does it matter? Let's just say that from now on I am in your
    hands.

29. EXT. STREET. NIGHT

ROSIE *runs into a shopping street. Chaos. A black man, accompanied by a white man and large crowd of assorted others, black and white, men and women, is about to smash a sledgehammer into the window of a hi-fi shop. The glass shatters. A cheer goes up. The crowd rushes into the shop. A young black man falls into the glass, getting up with his hands and face streaming blood. A TV crew films it all. The others grab electrical goods and flee with their loot through noise and chaos.* DANNY *stands there looking at* ROSIE, *with some of the straggly kids.* ROSIE *runs on. A little old white woman, with a shopping basket on wheels, rushes into the electrical shop and loots a transistor radio. She rushes out as fast as she can.*

30. INT. ROSIE'S STUDY. NIGHT

RAFI *lies in bed in the half-lit room. He's asleep, having a nightmare. He cries out, then awakes. He lies there being stared at by Virginia Woolf, which becomes more horrible the more she looks at him. The*

noise from outside rises around him. It could be in his head or for real:
he doesn't know. He sits up. On the edge of the bed he pulls cotton-
wool out of his ears. He covers his face with his hands.

31. INT. LIVING ROOM. NIGHT
SAMMY *is swigging a beer. An unnaturally large half-eaten*
hamburger and milkshake are on the table next to an open porn
magazine. SAMMY's *trousers are round his ankles. He's listening to a*
CD of something loud and noble – Shostakovich, for example. With
half a straw stuck up his nose he leans over a line of coke he's laid out
on the glass-topped table. Now RAFI *is at the door. He yells but cannot*
be heard above the music and SAMMY *sits with his back to him,*
having snorted the coke, bitten into the giant hamburger and eagerly
turned over a page of the magazine. Disturbed, SAMMY *turns to see,*
over the back of the sofa, his father gesticulating at him. Determinedly
RAFI *goes to the door of the flat, picking up his overcoat as he goes.*
SAMMY *stands up, trousers round his ankles, and falls over, the rest of*
his coke flying everywhere. He could try to snort it out of the carpet.
Cut to: SAMMY *stands at the top of the stairs pulling up his trousers as*
RAFI *runs downstairs.*
SAMMY: (*Yelling after him*) Haven't you got jet-lag, Dad?
RAFI: I have seen wars, you know!
SAMMY: Don't go out there, Dad!

32. EXT. STREET. NIGHT
RAFI *is now in the street and heading full-tilt towards the riot area.*
SAMMY *comes out of the house, hamburger and shake in hand, and*
down the street after him. There is much running about in the street.
The street is covered with debris. RAFI *stops by the car that* ROSIE *saw*
in flames. It is burnt out now but little flames unnaturally flicker all
over it.
RAFI: My God, I can't understand it, why ever do you live here?
SAMMY: It's cosmopolitan, Pop. And cheap. Come on. Let's go,
eh? Please.
RAFI: No, I want to see this.
(RAFI *pulls away from him. A young black man comes out of his*
house and runs down the street pursued by his father trying to stop
him going out. His mother stands at the door. Father and son
struggle.)

SAMMY: Leonardo da Vinci would have lived in the inner city.
RAFI: You know that for certain, do you?
SAMMY: Yes, because the city is a mass of fascination.
(*Now we see* RANI, VIVIA, EVA, MARGY, BRIDGET, *taking care of each other, watching the riot.* RANI *screams abuse at the violence of the police in dealing with people.* MARGY *is disgusted with the violence of the entire thing and by the sympathy of the other women for the rioters.*)
MARGY: But it's just men, rotten men, being men!
(EVA *is sympathetic to the rioters and carries an iron bar threateningly. Suddenly a brick comes from somewhere and smashes* VIVIA *in the side of the head. She goes down. The women gather round her. They pick her up and rush her away as a phalanx of police with riot shields makes towards them.* EVA *throws her iron bar at the police. As* SAMMY *and* RAFI *flee, we see injured people lying in the rubble, some attended by friends and ambulance people. A young white man squats under a hedge crying.*)
SAMMY: Rosie says –
RAFI: What does the great Rosie say?
SAMMY: Rosie says these revolts are an affirmation of the human spirit. A kind of justice is being done.
(*Pause. The situation becomes more dangerous. But* SAMMY *is excited.*)
Let's get the hell out of here!
(RAFI *stumbles. Now* ANNA *runs towards them, taking pictures. A bunch of white and black kids run past* RAFI.)
(*To* ANNA) What are you doing here, Anna? This isn't your part of town!
RAFI: These are fools and madmen!
SAMMY: (*As she photographs*) Anna, cut it out! This is my father!
ANNA: (*Shaking his hand*) Pleased to meet you, sir. Welcome to England. I hope you enjoy your stay! (*Kisses* SAMMY.) I'll give you a ring.
(*She goes. Cut to: Later.* SAMMY *is now hurrying* RAFI *back. Suddenly they turn a corner and stop beside a car. The windows have been smashed, the radio and speakers ripped out, etc. In the distance we see the backs of a line of police, as they charge the screaming mob.* SAMMY *is more concerned about the car and*

he kicks it wildly.)

SAMMY: For fuck's fucking fuck sake, fuck it!

RAFI: Boy, didn't they teach you more than one word at the school I paid through the arse for you to attend?

SAMMY: But this is my fucking car!

RAFI: Surely an affirmation of the human spirit?

(*Cut to:* SAMMY *and* RAFI *walk through gloomy reverberating alleys back to the house.* RAFI *has his arm around* SAMMY *now.*)

I don't want anything any more. The things I own are a burden to me. So I've given the factory to your cousins.

SAMMY: What, those idiots?

RAFI: They are going into air-conditioners. I think making heaters in one of the world's hottest countries was not good business sense.

(*Cut to: The steps of the house. On the steps an injured white kid is with his black girlfriend.*)

The money I've managed to get out of the country, and it's a lot of money –

SAMMY: Which total prick have you thrown that at, Pop?

RAFI: One of my main purposes in coming here is to transfer that money to your account, son.

(*Cut to: Now they are in the comparative silence of the stone hallway.*)

You can have the money provided you buy yourself a house in a part of England that hasn't been twinned with Beirut! Is there anywhere like that left? I would also like some grandchildren. Please. There is money for them too.

SAMMY: How much?

33. INT. OFFICE. MORNING

The office of an organization rather like Amnesty. VIVIA *and* RANI *sitting across the desk from a young Japanese woman.*

JAPANESE WOMAN: Rafi Rahman.

RANI: Yes, I rang you yesterday to ask for information.

(*The* JAPANESE WOMAN *rises, smiles.*)

JAPANESE WOMAN: I remember. Let me get the file to show you what we've got.

(*She goes.* VIVIA *and* RANI *hold hands nervously.*)

VIVIA: (*To* RANI) Suppose we find out some stuff about Rafi that

you wouldn't want to hear while you were eating your
breakfast? What do we do then – just tell Rosie and let her
get on with it?

RANI: Wouldn't it be worse to conceal something we knew?

VIVIA: I know, I know, but we'll be putting her in a difficult
position.

(*The* JAPANESE WOMAN *returns with a thick file and puts it
down on the desk.* RANI *and* VIVIA *lean forward to look at it.*)

JAPANESE WOMAN: That's volume one.

34. INT. LIVING ROOM. MORNING

RAFI *eats breakfast in his silk pyjamas. In front of him is his
chequebook. He has written the cheque and it lies on the table. Now he
writes a postcard. It is a few days later. He looks across the flat,
fascinated by the sight of* ROSIE *who, in a T-shirt and shorts, is doing
muscle-bursting vigorous weight-training and body-building exercises
to the sound of Mozart's Requiem.*

Cut to: A little later. ROSIE *is dressed for work now.*

RAFI, *walking about the flat, drops the postcard and bends over stiffly
to retrieve it.* ROSIE *picks it up for him.*

ROSIE: Writing home already? But you've only been here a few
days, Rafi. And you've hardly been out.

RAFI: Sweetie, read it. It's to my fondest relatives.

ROSIE: (*Reads:*) 'Streets on fire – wish you were here!'

RAFI: (*Pats her arse as she laughs.*) Rosie, one thing more. What
about the sound of little footsteps, eh? Isn't it about time?

ROSIE: (*Having to control herself*) Rafi . . .

RAFI: Eh? I know you're a kind of feminist, but you're not a
lesbian too, are you?

ROSIE: I'm thinking about having a child.

RAFI: (*Taking her hand*) It would give me so much happiness.

ROSIE: And that's exactly what I want, Rafi.

RAFI: You've cheered me up. I may even have the nerve to go out
today.

(*Cut to: A little later.* ROSIE *is leaving for work.* VIVIA *has
called round. She stands at the door with* ROSIE. VIVIA *gives*
ROSIE *a brown envelope.*)

VIVIA: This is from Rani.

ROSIE: Great. Thanks. (*Calls to* RAFI:) See you later, Rafi.

16

(Cut to: On the stairs down ROSIE *opens the envelope.* VIVIA *looks over* ROSIE's *shoulder.* RANI *has sent* ROSIE *material about* RAFI: *press cuttings from the Subcontinent and Britain: we can see his picture; photocopies of articles, Amnesty reports, etc.)*

VIVIA: Does Sammy know about all of it?

ROSIE: He's always tried to cut his father out of his mind. *(Pause.)* Poor Sammy.

35. EXT. STREET. MORNING

RAFI *is out for a walk. In his natty hat he passes through an alley with high walls and emerges into a run-down housing estate. One of those estates that looks a little like Soweto – no shops, no nothing.* RAFI *walks across the open area between graffiti-sprayed tower blocks. Kids roam around, some with scarves over their faces. Others wear crash helmets.*

Cut to: RAFI *has left the estate and turned the corner into another street, a main street. Here shops have been looted, burned out, the wrecked hulks of cars litter the place, paving stones discarded, etc. Plenty of onlookers, journalists, disconsolate shopkeepers, a film crew, street cleaners, etc.* RAFI *looks on. Now a white kid runs across the street carrying a hi-fi deck in his arms. He's followed by three cops. They all run incredibly fast. The kid drops the deck. The police grab him. A fight breaks out. Other people, both black and white, men and women, appear suddenly and pile in.* DANNY *stands watching on the edge of this. Someone is thrown against* DANNY *and he crashes back into the doorway. More police charge down the street.* DANNY *gets up and prepares to flee. As others run,* RAFI *can't get out of the way quickly enough, and gets knocked down. He falls to the ground.* DANNY *is tearing past him.* DANNY *stops though, picks* RAFI *up, and his natty hat, and pulls him away.*

Cut to: Breathless, DANNY *and* RAFI *have made it to an alleyway.* RAFI's *hands and knees are cut and grazed. He pulls up his trouser leg to examine the bloodied skin.* DANNY *takes* RAFI's *handkerchief, spits into it, and rubs* RAFI's *knee. There is noise all around them.* RAFI *is concerned about the state of his suit.*

DANNY: Where d'you live? Take you back home?

RAFI: Riot or no riot –

DANNY: Revolt. It's a revolt.

RAFI: Yes. Good. This society may be on its last legs but I am

expected in Cockfosters. Please point me north and say a
prayer in my favour.

(*A* TORY MP *and the* PROPERTY DEVELOPER *walk past the end
of the alley at this moment.* RAFI *and* DANNY *hear this.*)

TORY MP: You're a wealthy, intelligent businessman.

(DANNY *spits.*)

You've got to invest in this area – for your sake and ours.
You can do whatever you like.

PROPERTY DEVELOPER: I want that open space under the
motorway – then we can talk.

(*When they've gone* DANNY *pulls* RAFI.)

DANNY: Come on. I'll take you.

RAFI: Where?

DANNY: Come on.

36. INT. TUBE TRAIN. DAY

DANNY *and* RAFI *sit down,* DANNY *whipping away a newspaper
from the seat before* RAFI *sits down. Opposite them sits a huge white
man in a tracksuit. He is doing various finger-strengthening exercises.*
RAFI *watches him warily. Next to the* FINGER MAN *sits a woman,
middle-aged, off-white, with a wretched dog that eats a sandwich off
the floor. The woman has a cigarette in her mouth. And as she
scratches her ear the fag jumps from left to right in her mouth.*

RAFI: Do we have to change trains?

(*Suddenly the* FINGER MAN *rises up on the arm-rests of the seat.
And there he suspends himself like a fat bat. This is obviously
some kind of tube-train callisthenic.*)

FINGER MAN: (*To* DANNY) Time me, man!

(RAFI *practically has a heart attack as* DANNY *grabs his arm and
pulls his sleeve up to look at Rafi's watch. Meanwhile:*)

DANNY: (*To* RAFI) Danny, my name is. But people who like me
call me Victoria. People who don't like me call me jerk-off.
(*Pause.*) I know these tube lines. Sometimes I ride the tubes
all day. It's my office, the Victoria Line. It's where I do my
paperwork. Paperwork overwhelms me.

(*He glances over at the* FINGER MAN *whose face is about to
explode. He collapses back in his seat.*

Cut to: DANNY *and* RAFI *now walk together down a long tube
tunnel. As an expert, I suggest the tunnel that connects the*

*Piccadilly with the Victoria Line at Green Park – a superb
sensation you get here of endless walking in both directions. The
acoustics are excellent.*)

RAFI: I'm going to meet a woman – Alice – who I haven't seen for
over twenty years. I stayed in her house when I left
university. In those days before you were born there was a
colour bar in England. They gave me shelter, she and her
husband. Then I went back home to marry. But I . . . I loved
her terribly.

(*In the tunnel the straggly band of musicians are playing. We last
saw them crossing the motorway. They play the theme song of the
movie – there are trumpeters, saxophonists, a hurdy-gurdy player,
bassoon groovers, etc. Rappers. The dog from scene 2 is with
them. As DANNY and RAFI walk past, everyone in the band says
simultaneously, 'Wotcha, Danny boy.' DANNY nods regally.
Also, a couple of girls and boys are dancing to the music. If we
could film them from the front for a moment, we could easily see
for a second, the whole tube tunnel dancing, like in a Cliff
Richard film.*)

DANNY: Why didn't you get it on with her?

RAFI: My father wanted me to marry someone else. And Alice's
husband was watching me like a hawk. When I die and go to
heaven, I will marry her there.

DANNY: You don't know what she's like now.

(*The Asian CABBIE, in the brown suit, with the bandage over one
eye, walks towards them and on past them quickly.*)

37. EXT. STREET. DAY

*A leafy North London suburb, tree-lined, sedate, quiet. RAFI and
DANNY walk towards Alice's house – a detached four-bedroom place
with a front and back garden. RAFI has bought a large bunch of
flowers, a box of chocs and a bottle of champagne which DANNY
carries. Whites in the street stop and stare at RAFI and DANNY. RAFI
smiles politely at them.*

RAFI: Why are they looking at us like that?

DANNY: They think we're gonna rob their houses.

RAFI: God, things have changed so little! Poor Alice – she was
born and brought up in India, you know.

DANNY: She's black then?

RAFI: No, extremely white. But her family were in India for generations. I think I probably threw anti-colonial stones at her father's house in Bombay. (*They arrive at the house.*) This is it.

(RAFI *tries to get rid of* DANNY.)

OK then, Victoria. Be seeing you. Thanks.

(RAFI *pats him patronizingly on the shoulder and goes up the front path and rings the bell. He turns and sees* DANNY *standing halfway up the path.*)

DANNY: You won't make it alone out here in the country.

RAFI: This isn't the country, you damn fool. It's just respectable.

(DANNY *sees that* ALICE *has opened the door. He indicates to* RAFI. RAFI *turns, sees* ALICE, *and goes towards her. It is* DANNY *who is moved.* ALICE *and* RAFI *go into the house.* DANNY *stands there a moment, then goes round the side of the house.*

Cut to: Now DANNY *is in the back garden. An old white man and a mentally defective boy are doing Alice's gardening.*

Cut to: In Alice's living room RAFI *and* ALICE *sit on the sofa drinking tea. As they put their cups to their old lips we see their faces are streaming with tears although they talk normally. Alice's house is full of Indian memorabilia from the twenties and thirties. The walls are crumbling, everything is falling apart, it is a much stranger and darker place than it seems at first.*)

I'll never forget the kindness you showed me.

ALICE: But you did forget, Rafi. You forgot all about me.

(*Cut to: In the garden* DANNY *is walking about. He finds an old gardening hat on a bench which looks as if it's made from crushed budgie.*)

Sometimes when you were in the government there, I'd see you on the TV, talking about some crisis or other. You were impressive, though I did come to associate you exclusively with aeroplane hijackings. (*Pause.*) I thought you would come and see me before, you know.

(ALICE *has got up to put on a record, something romantic from the forties. When she sits beside him once more, they move into each other's arms.* RAFI *looks up to see* DANNY, *with the hat on, gazing through the window.* RAFI *becomes agitated, as you would. With his spare stroking hand he indicates that* DANNY

should disappear immediately. Just as ALICE *looks up,* DANNY's
face moves away.)
Shall I make some more Earl Grey tea? Don't be distressed,
Rafi. For me, you are still a charming and delightful man.
What about a piece of Jamaica rum cake?
RAFI: Alice, there's someone I think you should meet.
(*Cut to: The garden.* DANNY *stands there.* ALICE *and* RAFI
outside. ALICE *looks at* DANNY.)
(*To* ALICE) This is my map-reader and guide, Victoria. We
owe this visit to his ingenuity and kindness.
(*She greets him graciously.*)

38. EXT. SOUTH LONDON STREET. DUSK
A police car careers up the street. RAFI *and* DANNY *are crossing the
road on their way home.* DANNY *pulls* RAFI *out of the way of the
screaming police car.*
RAFI: (*To* DANNY) You nearly gave me a fucking heart attack
when I saw you outside Alice's window. (*Pause.*) What are
you doing now? Haven't you got anywhere to go?
DANNY: Yeah. I'm going with you.

39. INT. SAMMY'S AND ROSIE'S LIVING ROOM. DUSK
RAFI *and* DANNY *enter the flat.* DANNY *looks around.*
Cut to: We see DANNY *standing alone in the flat. He is clenching and
unclenching his fists, obviously distressed about something, unable to
get it out of his mind.* RAFI *comes up behind him.*
RAFI: Victoria, what's wrong?
DANNY: For a long time, right, I've been for non-violence. Never
gone for burning things down. I can see the attraction but
not the achievement. OK. After all, you guys ended
colonialism non-violently. You'd sit down all over the place,
right? We have a kind of domestic colonialism to deal with
here, because they don't allow us to run our own
communities. But if full-scale civil war breaks out we can
only lose. And what's going to happen to all that beauty?
RAFI: If I lived here . . . I would be on your side. All over the
world the colonized people are fighting back. It's the
necessity of the age. It gives me hope.
DANNY: But how should we fight? That's what I want to know.

40. EXT. SOUTH LONDON STREET. DUSK

SAMMY *waiting in the street.* ROSIE *walks through the crowd towards him.* SAMMY *stands drinking from a can of beer. Scenes of patched-up desolation around them. People are reconstructing their shops. Gangs roam about, watching. A heavy police presence. A* TORY MP *and the* PROPERTY DEVELOPER *stand in the street talking with their advisers.* ROSIE *goes to* SAMMY *and they kiss and greet each other warmly.*

ROSIE: Good day at the office, dear? I had only one suicide today.

> (*Cut to: Later. They are walking through the shopping area.*)

SAMMY: How's that dreary untalented prick?

ROSIE: Cut it out. Walter's got an exhibition.

SAMMY: Christ, a Renaissance man. Rosie, I think we should have a kid, you know. My seed's pretty rich at the moment – I've examined it. I'm well hot to trot in that respect.

ROSIE: But you wouldn't be a responsible father. The unfair sex has so far to go. (*Pause.*) Aren't you interested in politics any more? You were always out improving society, Sammy.

SAMMY: I find more and more that the worst thing about being on the left is the other people you've got on your side.

> (*She kisses him, holding him, laughing.*)

41. INT. ASIAN SHOP. DUSK

Now SAMMY *and* ROSIE *are in a wretched dark Asian shop on the front line. The Asian* SHOPKEEPER *is familiar to them. The shop was looted during the revolt. A white woman customer in the shop has a Siamese cat on her shoulder, on a lead.*

SAMMY: (*To* ROSIE) I can't see my old man staying too long, can you? (*To* SHOPKEEPER) Any noodles, Ajeeb?

ROSIE: You kissed your father on the nose and said he could stay forever.

SAMMY: You have to do that. It's a well-known lie.

SHOPKEEPER: The noodles are looking right at you.

SAMMY: So they are. Any Indian sweets?

> (SHOPKEEPER *shakes his head.*)

You're joking. You're not joking? Ajeeb, it's a terrible disgrace.

SHOPKEEPER: Samir, I tell you, the trash took everything in the looting. They're jealous of us. But why? In this country aren't we all in the same position?

22

ROSIE: (*To* SAMMY) Your father announced how long he wants to stay with us. (*Pause.*) One or two years, he said.

SAMMY: What?

42. INT. SAMMY'S AND ROSIE'S FLAT. EVENING

DANNY *has Sammy's huge TV in his arms and is staggering around under the weight of it. The TV is on and* RAFI *watches it with his feet in a bowl of water as* DANNY *perilously manoeuvres it into position for* RAFI. *This is to prevent* RAFI *from having to move.* RAFI *is watching footage of the riots on TV. He is wearing pyjamas and eating sherbets from a paper bag.*

43. INT. THE STAIRS UP TO THE FLAT. EVENING

SAMMY *and* ROSIE *walk up drinking, stop at the landing for an altercation and finally reach the door to their flat. They are getting on really well, despite everything.*

ROSIE: And did you see him filing his fingernails and –

SAMMY: Putting powder between his toes!

ROSIE: Or cutting the hair in his ears! D'you know he handed me his washing and said, 'Be sure not to use too hot an iron on the silk shirts!'

(ROSIE *and* SAMMY *crack up, leaning against the wall, laughing and slapping each other exaggeratedly.* SAMMY *stops abruptly.*)

SAMMY: Stop badmouthing my father, you silly bitch!

ROSIE: Oh fuck off.

SAMMY: I better tell you, Rosie. He's pretty keen to unload some dough on us. It's a lotta dough I'm on about here, darling. So we better get fucking respectful right now!

(*Cut to: Seconds later. They walk up,* SAMMY *behind, his hand up her skirt playfully.*)

ROSIE: We went to that factory where Rafi made his money, remember? I know Dante based the Inferno on it. You don't have to be radical to see that to accept one penny from him is to get into bed with all kinds of evil.

(*At the top of the stairs* ROSIE *fumbles for her keys but* SAMMY *leans lazily on the bell.*)

SAMMY: I don't think they come any more against inherited wealth than me, Rosie. But didn't Engels have a factory? (*She nods.*)

Right, let's take the money.

ROSIE: Sammy, I think you should know, your father was probably guilty of some other things too.

SAMMY: What things, beside paternalism, greed, general dissipation, mistreatment of my mother and vicious exploitation?

ROSIE: Well, he –

(DANNY *opens the door. He's holding a bottle of whisky and a glass.* DANNY *indicates for them to come into the flat. He pours a drink, which he gives to* ROSIE. SAMMY, *convinced they're being burgled, drops some of his shopping in fear. Through the open door* ROSIE *sees* RAFI *sitting there with his tired feet in the bowl.* ROSIE *smiles at* DANNY. DANNY *is now picking up* SAMMY'S *dropped shopping.* SAMMY *walks into the room and stares at* RAFI.)

RAFI: What's the matter, boy?

SAMMY: What the hell's going on?

(*Cut to:* DANNY *and* ROSIE, *bending down to pick up the shopping, look at each other with great interest.*)

ROSIE: (*To* DANNY) Live nearby?

DANNY: Not far. You?

ROSIE: Right here.

DANNY: What a thing.

44. INT. LIVING ROOM. EVENING

Later. The washing-up bowl has been removed. DANNY *and* RAFI *sit there watching TV.* SAMMY *walks uncomfortably around the room, drinking, trying to get rid of them.*

SAMMY: (*To* RAFI) I've gotta finish some accounts right now. And Rosie's got to get on with her writing.

RAFI: And what is Rosie writing?

(*By mistake* SAMMY *stands in front of the TV.* DANNY *stares affrontedly at him.*)

SAMMY: Oh sorry. (*To* RAFI) Yeah, she's doing a major article.

RAFI: On body-building?

SAMMY: Yeah. Kind of. It's on the ins and outs, the types, qualities and varieties of . . . It's a kind of historical socio-political investigation. Into kissing.

RAFI: Kissing? Speak up, son. Did you say kissing?

24

SAMMY: Yeah. 'The Intelligent Woman's Guide to Kissing in History.'

RAFI: Oh my God!

(DANNY *and* RAFI *catch each other's eye and laugh. Meanwhile* SAMMY *picks up the cheque his father wrote in the morning. He is impressed. He goes to his father and kisses him tenderly.*)

SAMMY: Thanks a double-bundle for this, Pop.

RAFI: (*To* SAMMY) I want to give you and my grandchildren everything I possess. Everything that is me. (*To* DANNY) And you, have you got any money? (*To* SAMMY, *indicating* DANNY.) Give him some damn dough.

(ROSIE *walks into the room, having showered and changed. She looks stunning.*)

Rosie, what is all this I hear?

ROSIE: About what, Rafi?

RAFI: Kissing. 'The Intelligent Woman's Approach'?

ROSIE: Snogging as a socio-economic, political-psychological-physical event sunk in a profound complex of determinations? Don't tell me that for you a kiss is just a kiss?

RAFI: Just a kiss.

(*She goes to* SAMMY *and kisses him on the mouth.*)

ROSIE: My husband. Our married mouths. That is one thing. It's meaning is clear. Now this –

(*She goes to* DANNY *and kisses him on the mouth. A long kiss. He almost falls off the chair.* SAMMY *and* RAFI *watch wide-eyed.*)

Now that's a different kind of kiss, with a different social and political meaning.

(*She takes a step towards* RAFI. *He cowers. She kisses him lightly on the mouth.*)

So as you all can see, there's so much to say on the subject of snogging you don't know where to begin.

(RAFI *laughs loudly in pleasure at her charm.*)

(*To* RAFI) Let's go out to dinner, eh? And how have you been today?

RAFI: Pretty well, in myself, despite the fact that several large people walked up and down on my head. Victoria saved me. Presumably this form of social exercise is an English custom now – a sort of Trooping of the Colour?

ROSIE: Yes, but less exciting for the working class.

(ROSIE *sees* SAMMY *glance again at the cheque before folding it and sliding it in his pocket.*)

SAMMY: Well, Victoria, won't your mother be wanting to know where you are?

(DANNY *gets up. He starts to walk towards the door.*)

RAFI: (*Quickly to* SAMMY *indicating* DANNY) Help him out. Please do what I say for once.

(SAMMY *reluctantly gives* DANNY *a fiver.* RAFI *nods at* SAMMY *again and he gives him, painfully, another fiver.* RAFI *nods once more.* ROSIE *is laughing, egging* RAFI *on.*)

(*To* ROSIE) But this is capitalism, Rosie. Redistribution once capitalism has created wealth, eh?

(DANNY *turns to go.* ROSIE *holds out her hands to him. He goes to her, shakes her hand, dropping the money in her lap. They look at each other.*)

SAMMY: Now, let's celebrate!

45. EXT. THE STEPS OF THE HOUSE. EVENING
The three of them stand on the steps looking out on the street. RAFI *has his arm round* SAMMY'S *shoulder.* SAMMY – *more or less unconsciously – pulls away from his father and takes* ROSIE'S *arm.* RAFI *is offended by this. They all walk down.*

46. INT. RESTAURANT. EVENING
ROSIE, SAMMY *and* RAFI *are eating in a smart expensive London restaurant. This is affluent, attractive London for a change. A string quartet of beautiful punks plays Mozart at the far end of the restaurant.* SAMMY *leaves the table a moment, excusing himself.*

RAFI: He hardly speaks to me, Rosie. Why doesn't he look after me and spoil his only father? Has he no feeling for me at all?

ROSIE: Why doesn't he carve miniatures?

RAFI: Perhaps he should. But why doesn't he?

ROSIE: Rafi, he doesn't know how to love you.

RAFI: Perhaps being ignorant of feelings helps him in his career.

ROSIE: He isn't completely ignorant of feelings. You did reject him.

RAFI: It was his ugly mother I rejected. I was made to marry her.

26

So I sent her to London and married again. You are very
loyal to Samir.

(SAMMY *rejoins them.*)

(*To* SAMMY) She is a decent woman. (*Pause. To* SAMMY) So
you got the nice cheque I gave you?

SAMMY: (*Nervous*) In my pocket, Daddio.

ROSIE: (*To* SAMMY) Let me have a look at it.

SAMMY: You know what a cheque looks like, don't you?
(*She nods.*)
Well, it's just one of those.

ROSIE: I want to know if you're going to return it to your father as
you said you would.

SAMMY: Why should I? Rosie, we're all set up now.

RAFI: (*To* ROSIE) Yes. Your principles annoy me and will pull
down my son.
(*There is a pause.* ROSIE *is furious with both of them.*)
Cheers to you all.
(ROSIE *admires a drag queen in the restaurant.*)

ROSIE: That woman is a real star.

RAFI: Now you're talking like a damn dyke.

ROSIE: (*To* RAFI) More wine? (*Pause.*) By the way –

RAFI: Yes –

ROSIE: Didn't a journalist who once described you as balding
have his teeth smashed in?

RAFI: (*Careful*) If his face had a mishap it improved his
appearance. (*To* SAMMY) Besides, his wife stole underwear
from Marks and Spencer's and lowered the reputation of my
country.

ROSIE: (*To* RAFI) When you were in the government there, people
– opposition people sometimes – were tortured and
murdered, weren't they?

SAMMY: Rosie, let's enjoy our meal.

ROSIE: I want him to answer. It's important.

RAFI: (*To* ROSIE) Sometimes. A little bit. It happens in the world.
It is necessary at times, everyone will admit that.
(RAFI, *finishing his meal, jabs his fork into a piece of meat on his
plate. As he raises it to his mouth we can see that it is a dead and
bloody finger with a long fingernail. We are aware of the people
at the next table, very straight yuppies in striped shirts and pearls,*

27

close enough to hear ROSIE. RAFI *places the indigestible*
fingernail on the side of his plate, delicately.)
ROSIE: Didn't they have to drink the urine of their gaolers?
(SAMMY *splutters into his drink.*)
Didn't you hang mullahs – religious people – upside down on
skewers and weren't red chillis stuck up their arses?
(*The yuppies call over the waiters.*)
RAFI: If they were, it was a waste of food. Let's have more wine.
Waiter!
SAMMY: (*To* ROSIE) I think Rosie wants to say that charm is no
substitute for virtue.
RAFI: (*Exploding*) Our government awoke the down-trodden and
expelled Western imperialists! I nationalized the banks! I
forged links with the Palestinians! Remember that! (*Irony.*)
Comrade. Khrushchev and I –
ROSIE: I just want to know –
(*The* MANAGER *hurries towards them.*)
RAFI: You know nothing but self-righteousness!
ROSIE: What does it feel like to kill, to torture, to maim, and what
did you do in the evenings?
MANAGER: Please, could you keep the noise down?
SAMMY:: Yes, I'm terribly sorry.
RAFI: I was imprisoned myself, you know! For ninety days, ill
with malaria, I didn't see sunshine! In the next cell lunatics
screamed. Their voices were even more irritating than yours!
ROSIE: You have increased the amount of evil in the universe.
RAFI: (*Furious*) You've never suffered! Never had to make hard
political decisions!
ROSIE: Yes, every day in my work!
RAFI: You are only concerned with homosexuals and women! A
luxury that rich oppressors can afford! We were concerned
with poverty, imperialism, feudalism! Real issues that burn
people!
ROSIE: We're only asking what it is like to destroy another life.
(*The* MANAGER *stands there beside them, angry himself.*)
MANAGER: Please –
ROSIE: (*To him*) All right, we're going!
RAFI: (*Pulling her towards him*) A man who hasn't killed is a virgin
and doesn't understand the importance of love! The man

who sacrifices others to benefit the whole is in a terrible position. But he is essential! Even you know that. I come from a land ground into dust by 200 years of imperialism. We are still dominated by the West and you reproach us for using the methods you taught us. I helped people for their own good and damaged others for the same reason – just like you in your feeble profession!

47. EXT. SOUTH KENSINGTON. NIGHT
They walk through South Kensington, from the restaurant to the car.
RAFI: (*Threatening*) Be careful what you say to me in the future, little girl. Remember who I am and have respect.
ROSIE: Who are you, Rafi? Who?
SAMMY: Rosie, he's my father.

48. EXT. SOUTH KENSINGTON. NIGHT
They have reached the car now. ROSIE *goes to the driver's side.*
RAFI: (*To* SAMMY) You'll be able to buy a new car for yourself now, eh? Rosie's car is good, but small.

49. EXT./INT. OVER THE RIVER. NIGHT
ROSIE *and* RAFI *in the front of the car,* SAMMY *in the back. They look at the Thames.*
RAFI: The river is ravishing tonight. But it must always be depressing to go back to that ghetto.
SAMMY: We try to entertain ourselves. And Rosie suggested the other day that we have a little party for you, Dad.
(ROSIE *swerves the car dangerously.*)
Yes, just a few friends, our and yours. Would you like that?
RAFI: That would be delightful. I must say, you have both been very kind to me – most of the time.

50. INT. LIVING ROOM. NIGHT
RAFI *stands on his head in a yoga position in his pyjamas.* SAMMY, *only a towel around his waist, carries two beers. He watches* RAFI *and walks across the room.*
RAFI: Nothing matters as long as you and I respect each other.
SAMMY: I know that.
RAFI: God bless you.

51. INT. SAMMY'S AND ROSIE'S BEDROOM. NIGHT

Continuous. ROSIE *doing stretching exercises in the bedroom, wearing a pair of blue silk pyjamas.* SAMMY *comes in.*

ROSIE: It was Rani and Vivia that got the information about your father.

SAMMY: There's all kinds of rumours about him! Some people say he gave hundreds of pounds to beggars in the street. Others say their relatives were bumped off! No one knows a thing for sure, Rosie, least of all you!

ROSIE: Sammy, you've got to face up to it and –

SAMMY: (*Cutting in*) Despite everything, Rosie, just admit it, he's a cheerful bastard with great spirit and –

ROSIE: (*Cutting in*) Sammy, listen to me –

SAMMY: Great generosity and optimism! He did miracles for that country. He was a freedom fighter.

ROSIE: (*Cutting in*) No, no, no!

SAMMY: We're just soft middle-class people who know nothing and have everything!

ROSIE: Just shut up and let me read this. Will you let me?

SAMMY: What is it?

ROSIE: You'll see.

(*Finally he nods and gets into bed.* ROSIE *picks up the brown envelope and reads from a testimonial given by a victim.*)

(*Reads:*) 'I will tell the truth of what prison was like there. On the first day they began to hit me on the back of my neck. Then they tied a wire around my testicles. A thin tube was pushed into my penis while someone forced a gun up into my arse, ripping the walls of my rectum until I was bleeding badly. I wanted to kill myself. Another man sat on my chest and stuck two fingers into each of my nostrils, tearing upwards until I thought I was going to choke. There were people I would willingly have betrayed. But I couldn't speak.'

(SAMMY *gets out of bed and goes to the door. He opens it and looks across the flat.* RAFI *sits at the table, reading a newspaper, listening to Wagner and drinking a glass of milk. He raises his glass to* SAMMY.)

(*Reads, as* SAMMY *looks at* RAFI:) 'Two soldiers would ask me a question and then push my head into a toilet overflowing

with human excrement. Later they taped adhesive over the
end of my penis so I didn't pee for five days. The pain got
worse and worse. I began to . . .'
(SAMMY *slams the door.*)
SAMMY: All right, all right!
(*He tears the paper from her hands.*
Cut to: Later that night. The living room. SAMMY *can't sleep.*
He listens to his father's contented snores at the door of his room.
He goes to the window and looks out on the street. The man in
the brown suit with the smashed head, the CABBIE, *lights a*
cigarette under a street lamp. SAMMY *turns and* ROSIE *is at the*
door to their room.)
What am I going to do? We did say we'd have a little do,
get some people round to meet him. We can't let a bit of
torture interfere with a party. But who will we invite?
ROSIE: We'll just have to round up the usual social deviants,
communists, lesbians and blacks, with a sprinkling of the
mentally sub-normal –
SAMMY: Yeah –
ROSIE: To start the dancing. And Victoria, yes?
SAMMY: I do love you more than anyone else I've known.
ROSIE: Me too, stupid. But we're both looking for a way out.
Aren't we, eh?

52. INT. LIVING ROOM. EVENING
SAMMY *is getting the flat ready for the little party. Furniture has*
been pushed back. SAMMY *is putting out food.* RAFI *stands there*
moving things away. He takes the key to the drawer out of the fruit
bowl. RAFI *opens the drawer, revealing a number of nasty-looking*
weapons: lumps of woods with nails in them, big spanners, etc.
SAMMY: We're gonna need more booze, Pop. You wouldn't
mind popping out, would you?
(SAMMY *notices the table drawer is open.*)
RAFI: I can feel that you've turned against me in the last few
days, even though your ignorance about me is profound.
But there's something you must hear me say. (*Indicates the*
weapons.) Look at this.
SAMMY: They're for self-protection. We're always getting
burgled. Those depraved deprived are right out of control.

31

RAFI: Yes, London has become a cesspit. You'd better come home, Samir.

SAMMY: I am home, Pop. This is the bosom.

RAFI: What a sullen young man you are. I mean, home to your own country where you will be valued, where you will be rich and powerful. What can you possibly like about this city now?

SAMMY: Well . . .

(Now we see a number of London scenes that SAMMY *and* ROSIE *like:* SAMMY *and* ROSIE *are walking along the towpath towards Hammersmith Bridge.)*

(Voice over) On Saturdays we like to walk along the towpath at Hammersmith and kiss and argue.

(Next we see SAMMY *and* ROSIE *in 'Any Amount of Books'.)*

(Voice over) Then we go to the bookshop and buy novels written by women.

(Next, SAMMY *and* ROSIE *outside the Albert Hall.)*

(Voice over) Or we trot past the Albert Hall and up through Hyde Park. On Saturday nights things really hot up.

(Cut to: outside the Royal Court Theatre in Sloane Square.)

(Voice over) If we can get cheap seats we go to a play at the Royal Court. But if there's nothing on that hasn't been well reviewed by the *Guardian* –

(Now we are in the small amused audience of a cabaret above a pub. This is the Finborough in Earl's Court. A man wearing a huge fat man's outfit, head disappeared into the neck, is dancing to an old French tune. (This is ALOO BALOO.) SAMMY *and* ROSIE *sit in the audience laughing and drinking.)*

(Voice over) We go to an Alternative Cabaret in Earl's Court in the hope of seeing our government abused. Or if we're really desperate for entertainment –

(We are now in the seminar room at the ICA. COLIN MCCABE *is talking to an enthralled audience about Derrida. A member of the audience has her hand up.)*

(Voice over) We go to a seminar on semiotics at the ICA which Rosie especially enjoys.

*(*ROSIE *also has her hand up. But* MCCABE *points to someone else.* ROSIE *looks at* SAMMY, *disgusted with* MCCABE'S *indifference to her.)*

32

AUDIENCE MEMBER: What, would you say, is the relation
   between a bag of crisps and the self-enclosed unity of the
   linguistic sign?
   (COLIN MCCABE *starts to laugh*.)
SAMMY: (*Voice over*) We love our city and we belong to it. Neither
   of us are English, we're Londoners you see.

53. INT. SAMMY'S AND ROSIE'S BEDROOM. EVENING
Minutes later. In the bedroom ROSIE *is now getting changed for the
party*. SAMMY, *agitated and upset by* RAFI, *watches her sexually*.
ROSIE: Did you give him the money back?
SAMMY: (*Wanting her*) Before I do anything, I need something to
   relax me.
ROSIE: (*Deliberately misunderstanding*) OK. Here's a couple of
   Valium.

54. EXT. STREET. EVENING
RAFI, *now out to buy booze, strolls across the street in his natty hat.*

55. INT. ROSIE'S AND SAMMY'S LIVING ROOM/BEDROOM.
EVENING
ROSIE *continues to dress. During this* SAMMY *combs her hair and puts
her shoes on. Through the open door of the bedroom we can see that*
RANI *and* VIVIA *have arrived. They have their arms around each
other. They sit and snog on the sofa opposite the bedroom. They've
brought the deaf and dumb boys with them.*
SAMMY: (*To* ROSIE) Why d'you think we don't want to screw
   now?
ROSIE: The usual reasons. Boredom. Indifference. Repulsion.
   (*Cut to:*)
VIVIA: Are they rowing?
RANI: Just talking each other to death.
VIVIA: No, listen, they're talking about sex.
RANI: Yes, but it's only heterosexual sex. You know, that stuff
   when the woman spends the whole time trying to come, but
   can't. And the man spends the whole time trying to stop
   himself coming, but can't.
   (*Cut to:*)
SAMMY: (*To* ROSIE) I wonder if it matters, us lying there night

33

after night as if the Berlin Wall had been built down the middle of the bed.

ROSIE: Don't ask me about sex. I know more about carrots. But I expect it's an acquired taste that one could do without.

SAMMY: You? Not you.

(*Cut to:*)

RANI: (*To* VIVIA) I'm always suspicious of those relationships where the couple have read about Simone de Beauvoir and Jean-Paul Sartre at too early an age. I want my partner to be on the rack or nowhere at all.

VIVIA: Kiss me, darling.

(*Cut to:*)

ROSIE: I've just started to enjoy screwing.

SAMMY: Christ, how can things become so strange between a common couple?

(*Cut to:*)

RANI: (*To* VIVIA) Rosie calls this household 'the hedgehogs'.

(VIVIA *looks at her.*)

Because there are so many pricks around.

(SAMMY *and* ROSIE *come out of their bedroom,* SAMMY *overhearing the last bit. They have their arms around each other.*)

SAMMY: Yeah but not all pricks are men.

56. INT/EXT. OFF-LICENCE. EVENING

RAFI *is in an off-licence across the street. The counter of the off-licence is separated from the shop by chicken wire, with a small gap for the money. Two Alsatians run up and down barking behind the counter. A huge white man, the* FINGER MAN *that we met in the tube, sits in the shop, a baseball bat beside him.* RAFI *buys booze and is pretty disturbed by the shop. The* FINGER MAN *fingers his bat, craning to watch* RAFI *as* RAFI *shops.*

Cut to: outside the off-licence we see DANNY *looking through the window at him.* DANNY *is with his girlfriend, the kid and the dog.* DANNY *indicates to his girlfriend to come and have a look. They peer through the glass at him. This makes* RAFI *rather uncomfortable.*

Cut to: RAFI *coming out of the off-licence.* DANNY *takes the booze from him.*

RAFI: Come on. You'd better come to a party.

57. INT. SAMMY'S AND ROSIE'S FLAT. EVENING

Now some guests have arrived. SAMMY *and* ROSIE *are together,*
RANI *and* VIVIA *with them.* RAFI, *now elegantly dressed, goes to*
SAMMY *and* ROSIE.

RAFI: Now you are together, tell me quickly: have you decided
to buy a house in Hatfield with the money I've given you?
(ROSIE, *irritated by him, just looks across the room and sees that*
DANNY *has arrived, among other guests.* DANNY *has the kid*
and the dog with him, OMAR *and* JOHNNY *are there too,*
JOHNNY *and* DANNY *talking. And then* ALICE *arrives.* RAFI
goes to her.
Cut to: Later on. The party swings. DANNY *stands by a sofa on*
which sit RAFI *and* ANNA. *Bits of conversation as we move*
across the room. RANI *and* BRIDGET *dance together, cheek to*
cheek. VIVIA *watches jealously.*)

RANI: I said to her, it's love this time, I want to be with you.

BRIDGET: I couldn't imagine being with anyone for more than
two weeks.
(ROSIE *watches* DANNY. SAMMY *watches* ROSIE. ANNA
watches SAMMY. OMAR *and an* ASIAN ACCOUNTANT *watch*
RAFI.)

OMAR: Sammy's our accountant. He never said his father was
Rafi Rahman. He kept that quiet.

ASIAN ACCOUNTANT: I was in Dacca when their army came in.
How d'you think my father was killed – falling out of bed?
(RAFI, *slightly drunk now – jacket off – has pulled up his*
polo-necked shirt and is showing ANNA *his scars.*)

RAFI: I'll show you my life!
(ANNA *peers interestedly at them.* RAFI's *stomach, chest and*
back are criss-crossed with long scars.)
(*Indicating*) The geography of suffering. Open-heart
surgery, gall-bladder, appendix, lung removal. It's a
miracle I am alive. Touch them.

ANNA: Are you sure?

RAFI: Treat yourself – the Kennedy children used to stay in my
house.

ANNA: I like men who try to impress me. They make me laugh.
(RAFI *looks up nervously and sees the white deaf and dumb boy*
staring at him. Cut to:)

JOHNNY: (*To* OMAR) If you had to sleep with anyone in this room who would you choose?

OMAR: (*Pause, looks around.*) Er . . . You.

(*Cut to:* ALICE *is talking to* VIVIA. *She also glances at* RAFI *and* ANNA, *a little disconcerted.*)

ALICE: Although I was curious about –

VIVIA: Other bodies –

(RANI *goes to* VIVIA *and kisses her warmly, looking at* ALICE.)

ALICE: Other men – and one is curious. And although I loved someone else – I loved Rafi – I was faithful to my husband. For no other reason than that we believed in not lying to each other. Loyalty and honesty were the important things for us. Not attraction. Not something called pleasure.

(*Cut to: Now* ROSIE *is with* DANNY.)

ROSIE: You look cool. (*Pause.*) Is it your kid? What's he called?

DANNY: Rosie, I missed you.

ROSIE: You don't know me.

DANNY: If I knew you it would have been worse.

(*Cut to:*)

ALICE: (*To* VIVIA) In that old world of certainty and stability you didn't take it for granted that a marriage would smash up in ten years. It was your entire life you gave to someone else.

(*Cut to:*)

ANNA: (*To* RAFI) I do Gestalt therapy, an hour of Indian yoga, followed by Buddhist chanting. Do you chant?

RAFI: Chant what, my dear?

ANNA: Mantras, to calm yourself.

RAFI: I am calm. It is agitation I seek. You young international people mystify me. For you the world and culture is a kind of department store. You go in and take something you like from each floor. But you're attached to nothing. Your lives are incoherent, shallow.

ANNA: I am for self-development above all. The individual reaching her fullest potential through a wide range of challenging experience.

RAFI: Ah yes. The kind of thing I used to call bourgeois indulgence in the days when I believed in reason and the struggle. My ideal evening then was a dialogue by Plato followed by women wrestling in mud.

36

(*Cut to:*)

ALICE: (*To* VIVIA) We didn't have exaggerated expectations of what sex and love could offer so we didn't throw each other over at the first unhappiness.

VIVIA: You didn't have your own lives. You lived through men. The penis was your life-line.

(ROSIE *and* DANNY *go off together, watched by* RAFI *and* ALICE.)

(*To* ALICE) Let's keep in touch anyway. Can we exchange phone numbers?

(*Cut to:* ROSIE's *study.* ROSIE *shows* DANNY *her books, drawings, etc. Now they hold each other. Their faces move closer together. Incredible sensuality, their hands in each other's mouths.*)

DANNY: Why don't we get out of this lonely place? And go to a lonelier one?

(*Cut to:* SAMMY *is with* RAFI *now.* ANNA *is photographing him.* RAFI *holds up his jumper, having a wonderful time.*)

RAFI: (*To* SAMMY) And where is Lady Chatterley?

SAMMY: Piss off. (*To* ANNA) What are you doing, please?

RAFI: I think I'm becoming a very free and liberated person.

(*Cut to:* SAMMY *stands disconsolately outside Rosie's study.* ANNA, *from the end of the hall, photographs him.* VIVIA *and* RANI *stand behind* ANNA *with their arms around each other.*)

SAMMY: Let's go, Anna!

(*We see* VIVIA *and* RANI *slip away.*)

58. INT. ROSIE'S STUDY. NIGHT
Seconds later. RAFI *is in his room, under the picture of Virginia Woolf. He's taking a couple of pills with a glass of whisky. He looks up – and the room is dark – and sees* VIVIA *and* RANI *standing there. They are not threatening him directly, but he is frightened.*

RANI: We wanted to talk to you, Mr Rahman.

VIVIA: Yes, if you don't mind.

RANI: About politics and things.

VIVIA: About some things that happened to some people.

RAFI: If I were you two girls, I'd –

VIVIA: Yeah?

(*Suddenly the door opens and* ROSIE *is standing there. The atmosphere is broken.* ROSIE *clocks the situation immediately and ensures that* RAFI *gets out.*)

ROSIE: Rafi, Alice is looking for you.

(RAFI *goes.*)

ROSIE: (*To* RANI *and* VIVIA) Please, not now.

RANI: But you do know who you have living in your flat?

ROSIE: I don't hate him.

RANI: Typically of your class and background. Your politics are just surface.

ROSIE: What do you want to do?

RANI: We want to drive him out of the country. (*To* VIVIA) This is liberalism gone mad!

(VIVIA *and* RANI *look pityingly at* ROSIE. *A hand appears on* ROSIE's *head. She looks up to see* DANNY *there.*)

ROSIE: (*To* DANNY) Ready?

DANNY: (*To* ROSIE) For anything.

59. INT./EXT. CAR OUTSIDE ALICE'S HOUSE. NIGHT

ALICE *is in the front of* SAMMY'S *new car, next to him.* ANNA *and* RAFI *sit in the back, the electric windows going up and down. The suburbs are silent.*

SAMMY: Anna, how d'you like me new car?

RAFI: (*To* ANNA) I bought it for him.

ANNA: And what does he have to do for you in return?

RAFI: Only care for me a little.

(ANNA *kisses* RAFI *goodbye, affectionately. He slides his hand up her skirt.*)

ANNA: You're quite an entertainment.

(*Cut to:* ALICE *walks towards her house, through the beams of the headlights.* SAMMY *and* RAFI *stand beside the car,* ANNA *inside. The car door is open and the music spills out into the street.* ANNA *can sing along with it.*)

RAFI: I'm staying here tonight because I want to be with Alice.

SAMMY: Now? At night?

RAFI: At all hours.

SAMMY: And on all-fours?

RAFI: The English waste their women. There's a good ten years' wear in Alice. You don't know what a good woman she is. In fact you don't know anything about women full stop.

SAMMY: What d'you mean, for God's sake?
RAFI: Where is your wife, for instance?

60. EXT. RAILWAY BRIDGE. NIGHT
ROSIE, DANNY, *the kid and the dog are crossing the railway bridge towards the waste ground. The kid and the dog run on, leaving* ROSIE *and* DANNY. *They stop and look over the bridge;* ROSIE, *never having seen the waste ground before, is startled and amazed. She watches the kids play chess on a huge iron-sculpted chess set. The players sit above the game like tennis umpires and order eager minions to move their pieces for them.* DANNY *is behind her, with his face in her hair. She tells him about herself.*
ROSIE: My father has a small furniture store and used to be the Mayor of Bromley! My mother was having an affair with the official chauffeur. I haven't spoken to Dad for five years. He's crude, vicious, racist and ignorant. I'd happily die without seeing his face again. I changed my name and became myself.
   (*She turns. They kiss a little.*)
DANNY: Are you going to come in for some hot chocolate?
   (*She nods. He takes her hand.*)
   Come on then, follow me up the yellow brick road.

61. INT./EXT. STREET. NIGHT
SAMMY *stops the car outside* ANNA'S *studio. She is still sitting in the back seat of the car, her arms around him, her hands over him. Her studio is in a working-class area of London now being taken over by the rich and the smooth.*
ANNA: Wouldn't you like to be with me tonight?
SAMMY: I'm trying to get on to a whole new regime.
ANNA: What for?
SAMMY: My prick keeps leading me into trouble. I'm like a little man being pulled around by a big dog.
   (*She touches him. He groans. He goes to get out of the car.*)
   Desire is pretty addictive though.

62. EXT. UNDER THE MOTORWAY. NIGHT
Here, on a large area of waste ground, is Danny's caravan. This is where he lives. There are many other caravans and shacks for the

39

straggly kids. Some of them – maybe Danny's – are decorated with
flashing Christmas lights. The traffic thunders overhead. ROSIE,
DANNY *waving a stick, the kid and the dog, walk towards the*
caravan. Kids in their teens and twenties, black and white, girls and
boys, stand around open fires or sit in old car seats, dragged out into the
open. Next to one fire, on a crate, is a huge TV which the kids watch.
On TV a headless man reads the news. On another part of the waste
ground, the straggly kids are playing a variety of instruments, the
stranger and more home-made the better, of course. Nearby, two cars
are half buried in mud, as if they plunged over the rim of the motorway
and nose-dived into the ground. A huge red Indian totem pole sticks up
into the sky. A swing hangs down from under the motorway. A kid
swings in it.

ROSIE: My father would smash me across the room. Then he'd
    put on his mayor's chain and open church bazaars. Since
    then I've had difficulty in coming to terms with men's
    minds. Their bodies are all right.

DANNY: The neighbourhood's busy tonight.
    (DANNY *and* ROSIE *walk up the steps into Danny's caravan.*)

63. INT. ANNA'S STUDIO. NIGHT
The light is strange and gloomy in the studio tonight. A lot of clothes –
lace, silk, velvet, leather – lying about from a photography session.
SAMMY *is very anxious, drinking, pacing about. She watches him,*
while putting various things in a bag: rugs, candles, cushions.

ANNA: You've got some bad anxiety, man. There are two types of
    people – or combinations of both at different times. Toxic
    and nourishing types. T and N. You're more T than N right
    now. It'll take more than that to stop me loving you. You
    better come with me.

64. EXT. FIRE ESCAPE. NIGHT
ANNA *is leading* SAMMY *up a fire escape at the back of the building.*
He stops. She pulls him on. She carries a bag.

65. INT. CARAVAN. NIGHT
In the large caravan, full of plants, pictures of Gandhi, Tolstoy,
Martin Luther King. DANNY *lies naked on the bed, reading a*
paperback. He looks desperately attractive. ROSIE *walks towards the*

bed and sees him. She stands and watches him, swigging from a bottle of cider, dancing a little. He throws the book aside. She is fully dressed. The dog stretches out on the floor.

ROSIE: Danny, God, you are gorgeous. Your legs. Head. Chest. You excite me. You're really doing it to me. Can you . . . would you do something? Just turn over.

(Unselfconsciously he turns over on to his stomach. ROSIE moves down towards him. And she touches him, moving her lips lightly over him.

Cut to: Outside, the band plays for the lovers and fires can be seen from the caravan windows. And of course inside the music can be heard.)

66. INT. ALICE'S BEDROOM. NIGHT

ALICE, *who has several Jane Austen novels beside her bed, is untying her hair in the crumbling eerie bedroom. Also, in this room, some Indian memorabilia. She wears a dressing-gown.* ALICE *looks at* RAFI.

RAFI: I like you in that dressing-gown. (*Pause.*) I'd like you out of it too. (*Pause.*) Do your kids come to see you?

ALICE: Once or twice a year.

RAFI: Is that more or less times than they go to the dentist?

ALICE: One works in the City. The other is in property.

RAFI: Rich?

ALICE: Of course, Rafi.

RAFI: The natural bonds are severed, though. And love is sought everywhere but at home. What is wrong with the home?

ALICE: Generally the people who live there. (*Pause.*) It's years since I've done this. And for you?

RAFI: (*Removing his trousers*) When I can . . . I like to.

ALICE: Like most women my life has been based on denial, on the acknowledgement of limits.

RAFI: Christ, Alice, let's just enjoy ourselves, eh?

(RAFI, cheerfully naked, is about to hang his clothes in the wardrobe. He catches sight of his own squat, hairy, wrinkled body in the wardrobe mirror. He jumps with shock. She laughs.)

ALICE: Never look in a mirror you don't know.

41

(*But he continues looking in the mirror. Standing behind him for a moment, he sees the* CABBIE *with the caved-in head.* RAFI *turns away and collects himself.*)

RAFI: Perhaps you're right. Right that we must contain and limit ourselves and learn to be content. The West has become very decadent, sex-mad and diseased since I came back. In my country you know what I did?

ALICE: Was it terrible?

RAFI: I shut all the night-clubs and casinos. The women have gone back in their place. There is restriction. There is order. There is identity through religion and a strict way of life.

ALICE: It is tyrannical no doubt.

RAFI: While here there is moral vertigo and constant change.

67. INT. CARAVAN. NIGHT

ROSIE *and* DANNY *lie on the bed in the caravan.* ROSIE *is half undressed now. Music from around the caravan. Their tongues dance over the other's face.*

ROSIE: In my kissing research I've learned that some people have hard tongues. Others, tongues that are too soft. You feel like sticking a fork in them. Others kiss so much like vacuum cleaners you fear for your fillings. But this is a kiss.

DANNY: I can't stop touching you.

ROSIE: Would you rather be writing a letter?

DANNY: I'm telling you something, Rosie.

ROSIE: I'm biting your neck. I love necks. Necks are mine.
(*And they wrestle a little.*)

DANNY: The woman who brought me up – because my mum was out at work all day – lived right near you. That's why I've watched you so often in the street.

ROSIE: Why didn't you say anything?

DANNY: I felt, well, that's quite a woman. But I thought: Victoria, you're well outclassed here. Until I realized that you're downwardly mobile!

ROSIE: What about the woman who brought you up?

DANNY: Paulette. The police just went into her house and shot her up. That was the start of the rebellion. Nobody knows the shit black people have to go through in this country.
(*We pull back to see, at the partition between the bed and the rest*

42

of the caravan, the kid standing there looking on.)

68. INT. ALICE'S BEDROOM. NIGHT
An old record plays on the gramophone in the room. ALICE *and* RAFI
*are in bed. She kisses him. She is releasing her hair, which until now
has been tied at the top of her head. He pulls away from her and her
hair tumbles free, all of it perfectly white, which shocks* RAFI. *Now
she reaches down to pull up her nightdress.*

ALICE: Women like Vivia are unnatural and odious, of course,
but there's something I've noticed about men that she would
understand. One is constantly having to forgive men. Always
they're wanting their women to see into them, understand
them, absolve them. Is there anything in that line you'd like
me to help you with, Rafi dear?

69. EXT. ROOF OF ANNA'S STUDIO. NIGHT
Here, overlooking London, the motorway nearby, are SAMMY *and*
ANNA. ANNA *is dancing for* SAMMY, *energetic, balletic, fluid,
soundless.* SAMMY *watches her. A helicopter passes over their heads,
the thick beam of its light illuminating them, the hurricane wind of its
propellers driving them into each other's arms.*

ANNA: You must be thinking about Rosie right now.
  (*He nods.*)
  How completely odd and freakish for a husband to think
  about his wife when he is with his lover.
  (*Suddenly she grabs him and pushes him violently towards the
  side of the building, thrusting him half over the low wall which
  separates the roof from the long drop.*)

SAMMY: What the fuck –

ANNA: How many lovers have you had in the past two years?

SAMMY: About . . . about . . .

ANNA: Yeah?

SAMMY: Twelve or so.

ANNA: For you pursuing women is like hang-gliding. They're a
  challenge, something to be overcome. It's fucking outta date,
  man! It's about time you learned how to love someone!
  (*She shoves him so we are looking straight down, with him.*)
  That's what fucking life is, baby!
  (*Cut to: He lies at her feet now, on the roof.* ANNA *has spread*

43

exotic rugs out and lit candles. There are also storm lanterns. He
massages her right foot.)
That's it, that point's directly related to my Fallopian tubes
. . . and there, that's my small intestine . . . yes,
diaphragm . . .
SAMMY: What would you do if you discovered that someone close
to you, a parent say, had done some stuff that was horrific
and unforgivable? They had ways of justifying it, of course.
But still it so disturbed you, you couldn't bear it?
ANNA: Your father? I don't know what I'd do, Sammy.
SAMMY: I don't know either, you know.
ANNA: Come here.
(*She indicates to* SAMMY *and he goes to her. They hold each other
and roll away across the roof.*)

70. INT./EXT. COLLAGE OF COPULATION IMAGES. NIGHT
*Now there is a collage of the three couples coupling. This is cut with
the kids and the straggly band outside the caravan dancing in
celebration of joyful love-making all over London. Some of the
straggly kids play instruments or bang tins. Others are dressed in
bizarre variations of straight gear – like morris dancers, pearly queens,
traffic wardens, naval ratings, brain surgeons, witches, devils, etc.
The cinema screen suddenly divides vertically (or would it be more
appropriate horizontally?) and we see the three couples in energetic,
tender and ecstatic climax, with* DANNY *and* ROSIE *in the centre.*

71. INT./EXT. WASTE GROUND. MORNING
ROSIE *has woken up alone in the caravan. She goes out of the
caravan. The straggly kids, with* DANNY *and his kid, are having
breakfast outside. They eat at a long table set out in the open, the
motorway above them. In the daylight* ROSIE *can see the kids have
planted vegetables in the waste ground and a young black woman
walks up and down with a watering can with a dildo-penis for a
funnel. A number of sculptures have been built in the vegetable patch.
In the background a shop has been set up in an old shack. Here
customers buy vegetables, books, etc. On the long table* ROSIE *sees a
printing press has been set up and the kids run off pages for books
they're printing.* ROSIE *sits down next to* DANNY *and has breakfast.
When she looks to the periphery of the site, beyond the barbed wire, she*

44

sees three white men standing in the open back of a lorry. One of
them has a pair of binoculars. They watch the kids.

ROSIE: (*To* DANNY) What's going on?

DANNY: They're chucking us off this site – either today, the
next day or the day after that.

72. INT. ANNA'S STUDIO. MORNING

ANNA *is asleep.* SAMMY *goes to* ANNA *with a tray – on it are
croissants, juice, eggs and coffee. He kisses her and she opens her eyes.*

SAMMY: Let's look at the photographs you took of that place I
want to buy.

(*Cut to: A little later.* ANNA *and* SAMMY *sit on the bed.* ANNA
*shows him photographs of a smart and inhabited house in
Fulham. Wittily, she has photographed the ridiculous yuppie
inhabitants showing the place off.*)

Which'll be Rosie's room?

ANNA: I'm having an exhibition in New York. I'm going to call
it 'Images of a Decaying Europe'. So I should photograph
that black guy at the party. D'you know where he is?

SAMMY: On top of my wife I expect.

73. INT. ALICE'S LIVING ROOM. DAY

ALICE *and* RAFI *are sitting at the table having breakfast. They've
almost finished.* RAFI *is eager to leave.*

ALICE: What would you like to do today?

RAFI: (*Rising, wiping his mouth*) I think I'd better get moving,
Alice. Sammy and Rosie will be expecting me.

ALICE: Why should they be expecting you? You really want to
go, don't you? Is there anything you have to urgently do?
I'd just like to know.

RAFI: Alice. I want to start writing my memoirs.

74. INT. SAMMY'S AND ROSIE'S FLAT. DAY

RAFI *has returned. The flat looks wrecked from the night before.*

RAFI: Sammy! Sammy!

(RAFI *goes into Rosie's study. Hearing a noise in the bedroom
he opens the door and sees* RANI *and* VIVIA *in bed. He is very
shocked and angry. He starts to abuse them in Punjabi. This is
sub-titled.*)

What are you doing, you perverted half-sexed lesbians
cursed by God?

RANI: Fuck off out of it, you old bastard!

RAFI: God save my eyes from the sights I'm seeing!

(*He shuts the door and cowers behind it as* RANI *and* VIVIA *throw
stuff at him.*)

RANI: (*Raving at him*) Come here and let me bite your balls off
with my teeth and swallow them! I'll rip off your prick with a
tin opener! I'll sew live rats into the stomach of your camel,
you murdering fascist!

(*As she throws books at him:*) Who the fuck do you think
you are! (*Now she is opening the drawer and removing the
weapons.*) That pigshit bastard, I'll crush his testicles right
now!

(*As she lunges with her piece of wood at him:*)
Let me get at that withered sperm-factory with this and put
the world out of its misery!

(*And she bangs wildly on the door of the room. We see* RAFI
climbing out of the window.)

75. EXT. OUTSIDE SAMMY'S AND ROSIE'S HOUSE. DAY

RAFI *is climbing down the drainpipe. When he looks down he sees the*
GHOST *looking up at him. Along the street* ROSIE *is getting off the
back of Danny's motorbike.* RAFI *jumps the last few feet to the ground,
damaging his arm as he falls. The* GHOST *walks away backwards,
watching him.* RAFI *walks towards* ROSIE *and* DANNY. *He sees them
warmly embrace. The police in the street look on in disgust.* RAFI *is
furious, on Sammy's behalf, with* ROSIE *and* DANNY. DANNY *spots*
RAFI *over* ROSIE'S *shoulder. He calls out to* RAFI *as* RAFI *tries to slide
past unnoticed, concealing his damaged arm.*

DANNY: Hey Rafi, why don't you come by for a talk sometime?
I'd like to see you.

RAFI: I don't know where you live, Victoria.

DANNY: Here, let me draw you a map.

(DANNY *goes over to his bike for pen and paper.* RAFI *and* ROSIE
are to one side.)

ROSIE: (*Wickedly*) Up all night?

(RAFI *looks back at the house and sees* RANI *and* VIVIA *standing
on the steps watching him.* BRIDGET *approaches* RANI *and*

46

VIVIA, *and they talk briefly, indicating* RAFI.)

RAFI: (*To* ROSIE) What the hell are you doing kissing this street rat and bum Danny on the road!

ROSIE: I find that rat bums have an aphrodisiac effect on me, Rafi.

(DANNY *goes over with the map and gives it to* RAFI.)

DANNY: See you then.

RAFI: I was adored once, too.

(RAFI *walks away.* BRIDGET *comes down the steps of the house and follows him.* DANNY *and* ROSIE *embrace to say goodbye.*)

ROSIE: (*To* DANNY) You're fond of that old man, aren't you?

DANNY: It's easy for me to like him. But it's you that makes my bones vibrate.

ROSIE: Uh–huh. (*Pause.*) I'd better go. Or Sammy will be anxious.

76. INT. THE TUBE. DAY

RAFI *is lost in the tube. He is standing in the ticket area of somewhere like Piccadilly with all the people swirling around him.* BRIDGET *is watching him. A group of young Jewish kids are being harangued by a group of young men. They yell: 'Yiddo, yiddo, yiddo!' at the kids.* RAFI *is confused and lost.* BRIDGET *is whispering to* EVA. *And* EVA *follows* RAFI *from now on, as he decides to go down a tube tunnel.*

77. INT. SAMMY'S AND ROSIE'S FLAT. DAY

SAMMY, *in a good mood, has come home.* ROSIE, *alone in the flat, is sawing the legs off the bed, as it's too high. When she hears* SAMMY *she goes into the living room. He kisses her. But she is in a very bad mood.*

SAMMY: Where's Daddio?

ROSIE: He went off somewhere.

SAMMY: You didn't offend him, did you?

ROSIE: Offend him?

SAMMY: Yeah, you know, 'What's your favourite torturing method out of all the ones you know?'

ROSIE: He's been here long enough.

SAMMY: We can't just chuck the old fucker's arse out on to the street. What'll he do, become a busker?

ROSIE: Why, does he play a musical instrument? It's not as if he's poor, is it?

SAMMY: It is. We've got his money. And there are people who want to kill him. Listen, I've seen a house which would suit both of us bunny rabbits. So much room we could go for days without seeing each other. Or without seeing Pop.

ROSIE: Your father?

SAMMY: He could have the basement, or dungeon, as we could call it.
(*She turns away from him, unable to share his ebullience.*)
Let's try and love each other a little. Can't we try to touch each other or something?

ROSIE: How did you enjoy sleeping with Anna last night?

SAMMY: To be honest, I'd rather have stayed in and redecorated the kitchen. You? (*Pause.*) You're smiling inside at the thought of Danny. Did you like each other?

ROSIE: He excited me terribly.

SAMMY: And the traffic didn't get on top of you?

78. EXT. OUTSIDE ALICE'S HOUSE. DAY
RAFI *walks towards the house.*

79. INT. ALICE'S BATHROOM. DAY
ALICE *in the bathroom bandaging* RAFI'*s damaged arm.*

RAFI: I can't live in that part of London. That's why I came back. Day after day those kids burn down their own streets. It's hard on tourists like me.

ALICE: (*Shocked, indicating arm*) Is that how this happened – in a mad riot?
(RAFI *nods and tries to kiss her. She turns away from him. Cut to: They walk down the stairs,* RAFI *in front.*)
I hate their ignorant anger and lack of respect for this great land. Being British has to mean an identification with other, similar people. If we're to survive, words like 'unity' and 'civilization' must be understood.

RAFI: I like rebels and defiance.

ALICE: You funny little fraud, you shot your rioters dead in the street! The things we enjoy – Chopin, Constable, claret – are a middle-class creation. The proletarian and theocratic ideas

48

you theoretically admire grind civilization into dust!
(*At the bottom of the stairs, in the hall,* RAFI *tries to hold her. She evades him.*)

RAFI: Please.

ALICE: What is it, Rafi?

RAFI: Sammy and Rosie have no human feeling for me. It would be terribly painful to have me living here?

ALICE: You couldn't leave quickly enough this morning. There was barely a heartbeat between your eyes opening and the tube doors shutting!

RAFI: I know, I know. Alice, take pity on me. I've got a lot of personal problems.

ALICE: (*Taking his hand*) Come. Let me show you something now.

80. INT. CELLAR. DAY

ALICE *takes* RAFI *through a door in the hall and down the perilous stairs into the gloomy cellar of the house. The place is stuffed full of old furniture, boxes, files, more Indian memorabilia – mosquito nets, hockey sticks, old guns. As* RAFI *follows* ALICE *through all this, picking his way to the far end, he sees that the* GHOST *is in the cellar with him, walking immaterially through objects. To turn away from this frightening sight, he turns to look at a framed picture. This is of Alice in India as a baby, with her ayah – the Indian servant who would have brought her up.*

ALICE: That's me as a baby, with the ayah that brought me up for the first eight years of my life
(ALICE *is taking down an armful of large dusty notebooks from the shelves at the end of the cellar. Accompanied by the* GHOST RAFI *goes to her as she opens the notebooks.*)

RAFI: What is this, Alice?
(*As she flips slowly through them we can see there is an entry for each day through the years 1954, 1955, 1956. Each entry begins 'Dear Rafi . . .' or 'My Darling Rafi . . .' or 'Dearest Rafi . . .'*)

ALICE: Every day for years as I waited for you, I poured out my heart to you. I told you everything! Look, pages and pages of it! I really waited like a fool for you to come back and take me away, as you said you would. Look at this.
(*She goes to an old suitcase, covered in dust. With difficulty she*

49

opens it. The GHOST *watches* RAFI.)
It's thirty years since I closed this case.
(*Slowly she pulls out and holds up the rotting garments.*)
These are the clothes I packed to take with me. The books.
The shoes. Perfume . . .

RAFI: Alice . . .

ALICE: I waited for you, for years! Every day I thought of you!
Until I began to heal up. What I wanted was a true marriage.
But you wanted power. Now you must be content with
having introduced flogging for minor offences, nuclear
capability and partridge-shooting into your country.

RAFI: (*To the* GHOST) How bitterness can dry up a woman!

81. EXT. OUTSIDE ALICE'S HOUSE. DAY

RAFI *leaves* ALICE'*s house. From the door she watches him go.*

82. INT. SAMMY'S AND ROSIE'S BATHROOM. DAY

SAMMY *and* ROSIE *in the bath together.* SAMMY *shampoos* ROSIE'*s
hair.*

ROSIE: Soap?

SAMMY: No, I already washed today. (*Pause.*) Where can the old
man have got to?

ROSIE: Sammy, this is all false, isn't it? I think we should try not
living together. I think we should try being apart now.

83. EXT. SOUTH LONDON STREET. DAY

RAFI, *with his bandaged arm and disintegrating map (that Danny
drew for him), walks through the desolate tunnels and grim streets of
South London. Now it is raining.* RAFI *stops under a railway bridge
where other wretched rejects are sheltering – the poor, the senile, the
insane, the disabled. Some of them sleep in cardboard boxes, others in
sleeping bags.* RAFI *trips over someone. He turns to them. During all
this, the Indian in the filthy brown suit, with a scarf over his head, the*
GHOST, *is watching him. Further away,* EVA *watches* RAFI *with*
MARGY.

RAFI: (*To man*) Will you pull off my shoe?
(*The man, who is black, tries to pull* RAFI'S *shoe off.
Cut to: Now* RAFI *walks on. The brown-suited man follows him,
carrying* RAFI'S *discarded shoe.*)

50

Cut to: Now RAFI *is walking in another part of South London in the pouring rain. Soaked through, bandage dangling, he is approaching the waste ground. In the street two bulldozers are being driven to the site. Around the perimeter of the waste ground several big cars are parked. White men, in suits, look at the site, talk about it, and point to things. The Indian in the brown suit, the* CABBIE, *looks on.* RAFI *walks past the nose-dived cars, ankle deep in mud. One of the kids – the one whose mother was shot at the beginning of the film – points out Danny's caravan to him. Music blares out over the waste ground.* RAFI *goes to Danny's caravan and bangs on the door.*

84. INT. DANNY'S CARAVAN. DAY

RAFI *stumbles into the caravan.* DANNY *sits writing at an old typewriter. A young black woman stands on a chair playing keyboards. The keyboard is slung over her shoulder like a guitar. They look up at* RAFI. DANNY *goes to* RAFI *and holds him up.*

RAFI: I thought I'd take you up on your offer of tea. Is it real or tea-bags?
  (*Cut to: Now* DANNY *is making tea. The woman plays the keyboards. A white rabbit runs around the caravan.* RAFI *looks around the place and at the pictures.*)
  You really live here all the time? Like you it's the middle class I hate.

DANNY: This land's been bought by the property people. The government's encouraging fat white men with bad haircuts to put money into the area.

RAFI: When we first met, you and I, in the street, you were very kind to me. I'll never forget it.

DANNY: Yeah, an old woman I loved got shot up by the police. Friends of ours were pulling whites out of cars and beating them in revenge. I didn't know if I should be doing it.
  (DANNY *gives* RAFI *his tea.* RAFI *looks behind him out of the window into the pouring rain. The leaves of the drenched bushes frame* RAFI'S *view of the brown-suited man who stares through the window.*)

85. INT. SAMMY'S AND ROSIE'S LIVING ROOM. EVENING

ROSIE *is helping* SAMMY *learn to stand on his head. Now he is up.* ROSIE *holds him up straight.*

ROSIE: If you had to choose between sleeping with George Eliot or Virginia Woolf, who would you choose?

SAMMY: On looks alone, I'd go for Virginia. Now you. De Gaulle or Churchill, including dinner, full intercourse and blow job.

ROSIE: (*Pause. Thinks, then:*) If we don't live together, if we live with other people, if we do entirely different things, I won't stop loving you.

SAMMY: That's not enough. We've got to be committed to each other.

ROSIE: It's not commitment you want. It's fatal hugging that you're into.

SAMMY: Rosie, where's the old man? D'you think he's gone back to Alice's for a second helping of trifle? (*Pause.*) Danny or me?

ROSIE: That's easy.

86. EXT. THE WASTE GROUND. NIGHT

A meeting is taking place. The kids and RAFI *sit around a huge bonfire discussing what they should do. Around the perimeter fence the bulldozers, the* PROPERTY DEVELOPER *and his cronies are discussing what to do. Some kids play music.*

DANNY: (*To the group*) They'll remove us tomorrow morning.

KID: (*To the group*) What do people think we should do?

KID TWO: Not go without a fight.

KID THREE: Go peacefully. We're anarchists, not terrorists.

KID FOUR: (*To* RAFI) You're a politician. What do you think?
(*Sitting among the kids, the man in the brown suit watches. The kids look at* RAFI *respectfully.*)

RAFI: We must go. The power of the reactionary state rolls on. But we must never, ever be defeated.

87. EXT./INT. THE WASTE GROUND/CARAVAN. NIGHT

It is late. Everyone is asleep. The Asian in the brown suit, the GHOST, *has walked across the silent waste ground to Danny's caravan. Outside he removes his suit until he is naked.*
Cut to: Inside the caravan RAFI *has got up from his bed to wash his face. He runs water into the bowl. He has his back to the door of the caravan. As he washes suddenly the bowl is full of human blood and*

52

hair and bone. A noise behind him. RAFI *turns and sees the* GHOST *covered in blood and shit, with serious burns over his body. The body is criss-crossed with wires from the electric shock treatment he received in detention. Over his head he wears a rubber mask through which it is impossible to breathe. He makes a terrible noise.* RAFI *turns and stares. The* GHOST *removes his rubber mask. We can see now that the head is half caved in and one eye (with the bandage removed) has been gouged out.*

GHOST: I'm sure you recognize me, though I don't look my best.
    (RAFI *nods. The* GHOST *sits on the bed. He pats the bed next to him.* RAFI *has got to sit next to him. The* GHOST *puts his arms around* RAFI. *Then the* GHOST *takes the pads connected to the wires which are stuck to his temples and puts the two of them over* RAFI'*s eyes.*)
    You said to Rosie that I was the price to be paid for the overall good of our sad country, yes?

RAFI: Forgive me.

GHOST: How could that be possible?

RAFI: Since, I have tried to love people. And it wasn't I who did the mischief! I wasn't there, if it happened at all!

GHOST: You were not there, it is true, though you gave the order. You were in your big house, drinking illegally, slapping women's arses adulterously, sending your money out of the country and listening, so I heard, to the songs of Vera Lynn.

RAFI: The country needed a sense of direction, of identity. People like you, organizing into unions, discouraged and disrupted all progress

GHOST: All of human life you desecrated, Rafi Rahman!
    (*The* GHOST *raises his arms. Now the caravan is plunged into darkness.* RAFI *screams. Electricity buzzes.*)

88. INT. ALICE'S LIVING ROOM. MORNING
The following morning. ALICE *is on the phone.*

ALICE: (*To* VIVIA) I'm a little worried about him, Vivia. Do you know where he is? Oh good. Yes I'd like to see him. (*Writes on a pad.*) I'll be there.

89. EXT. THE WASTE GROUND. MORNING
Around the perimeter fence the bulldozers are in place. The property

53

developer's men are arriving. They discuss how to do the job. Some of the kids are spreading cloth, wool, cotton, and large areas of brightly coloured material over the barbed wire. In their caravans and trucks other kids are packing up. The GHOST *in the brown suit leaves Danny's caravan.*

90. INT. SAMMY'S AND ROSIE'S LIVING ROOM. MORNING
SAMMY *is separating the books. Rosie's are left on the shelves – Sammy's go into boxes.* ROSIE *comes into the room. She is just about to go out.*

ROSIE: Sammy, what are you doing?

SAMMY: Getting ready to leave, now the decision has been made. (*Continues, not bitterly.*) That's mine. Mine. Yours, mine. (*Holds up* The Long Goodbye.) Mine?

ROSIE: No, I bought it. When we were at college.

SAMMY: I bought it for you.

ROSIE: Whose does that make it, officially? Oh, you take it. We read it to each other in Brighton. We made love on the train. (*Pause.*) I've got to go. They're being evicted today. Any news on Rafi?

SAMMY: I wondered why I was feeling so cheerful – I haven't thought about him today. I'll find him this morning.

91. EXT. THE WASTE GROUND. DAY
Now the exodus has begun. The caravans are starting to move; the fence has come down. The PROPERTY DEVELOPER *and his men are moving over the site with dogs. Police accompany them. The heavies smash down the shop to clear the way. The heavies hustle the straggly kids. Caravans get stuck in the mud. Some kids are trying to dig them out.* DANNY *is at the wheel of one of these trailers. The bulldozers start to move across the waste ground, clearing the debris, flattening the earth. The* PROPERTY DEVELOPER *stands in the back of an open-roofed car yelling instructions through a megaphone. The kid whose mother was shot (*MICHAEL*) is defiant, shouting at the heavies and the police who accompany them.*
Cut to: Inside Danny's caravan. RAFI *lies moaning on the bed. Frightened by the caravan's movement, he staggers to the door.*
Cut to: Opening the door of the slowly moving caravan, we see RAFI's *view of the waste ground. We see the convoy moving slowly*

54

off, kids being pushed around, trying to organize themselves.
Cut to: On the periphery, being held back by the police, is ROSIE, *and with her* VIVIA, RANI, EVA. *A woman in a long sable coat is watching the action – the property developer's wife.* RANI, *standing beside her for a moment, sprays a cross in green paint on her back.*

VIVIA: (*To* ROSIE) Your father-in-law has finally joined the proletariat.

ROSIE: What? Is he here?

RANI: Somewhere.

    (ALICE *has arrived now. We see her getting out of her car and walking through the police to* ROSIE, RANI, VIVIA. *She watches the police brutally arresting young women. She is shocked by this. She takes* VIVIA's *arm. The other women try to move forward, along with a lot of the other spectators. They are obstructed by the heavies and police. The* PROPERTY DEVELOPER *in his jeep rides past yelling through his megaphone.*)

PROPERTY DEVELOPER: Here we go, here we go, here we go! Fuck off, you lesbian communists!
    (*Then he recognizes* ALICE *and she him. He stops.*)
    Alice, what brings you here?

ALICE: (*Indicating everything*) Is this you, Norman?

PROPERTY DEVELOPER: Yes, I'm proud to say – making London a cleaner and safer place.

ALICE: I'm after someone. Can I get through a minute?
    (*He waves* ALICE *through.*)

PROPERTY DEVELOPER: How's Jeffrey?

ALICE: Probably I see my son less than you!
    (*As* ALICE *goes through on to the site,* ROSIE, VIVIA, EVA, RANI, *etc., accompany her. The* GHOST, *walking away in the opposite direction, slips in the mud and, unnoticed by anyone but the kid whose mother was shot, goes under the wheels and is broken. By now* ANNA *has arrived on site. We see her moving around quickly, photographing where she can without getting hurt.* ALICE *has reached* RAFI, *who is staggering around in the mud.*
    Cut to: Wider shot of the convoy moving away. ALICE *is taking care of* RAFI. *He is in a terrible state.* ROSIE *joins them.*)

ROSIE: (*To* ALICE) Come on, let's get him out of here. Take him to my place.

(RANI *watches this and* ROSIE *sees her.*
*Cut to: The convoy is leaving the waste ground and heading for
the road. The kids remain defiant, cheerful and rebellious, like
the PLO leaving Beirut. Some of them sit on the top of the
moving caravans, playing music as they go.*
Cut to: ALICE *walks away with* RAFI, *supporting him as they go.*
RAFI *is raving.*)
RAFI: I'm not leaving! Take me back! We must not allow those
fascist bastards to drive us away! We must fight, fight! (*To*
ALICE) You've never fought for anything in your damn life!
(*She gets* RAFI *in the car. He collapses in the back. She is very
upset by what has happened to him.*)

92. EXT. MOTORWAY. DAY

SAMMY, *who is driving to Alice's, heads along the motorway. He
stops the car, gets out. On the waste ground, looking up, we can see*
SAMMY *standing on the rim of the motorway, watching it all. He calls
and shouts down to* ROSIE. *He shouts with all his might.*
SAMMY: Rosie! Rosie! Rosie! Rosie!
(*But of course she doesn't hear him.* ANNA *notices* SAMMY,
though. She looks up and waves. DANNY *shouts to* ROSIE *from
the truck.*)
DANNY: Looks like I'm on my way out!
(*A final shot, later: The convoy having left, the bulldozers doing
their work, the waste ground having been cleared, we see* ROSIE,
VIVIA *and* RANI *walking across the waste ground.* VIVIA *carries
the black anarchist flag which fell from the top of one of the
caravans.*)

93. INT. SAMMY'S AND ROSIE'S FLAT. DAY

It is later that day. The women – taking RAFI *with them, have gone to
Rosie's flat to discuss the morning's events.* RAFI *is in the study. The
women,* RANI, VIVIA, ALICE, ANNA, ROSIE, BRIDGET, *eat and
talk.*
RANI: The way Danny's lot were treated shows just how illiberal
and heartless this country has become –
ALICE: But they were there illegally –
ANNA: Surely they'd been there for so long, though –
(*We get the flavour of their intense and good-natured*

56

conversation. As it continues, we move across to see RAFI
*watching them from his room a moment, before shutting the door
of the study. Now we are in the room with him. The conversation
from the living room can continue over, muffled.*)

ALICE: It doesn't affect the law. The law is to protect the weak
from the strong, the arranged from the arbitrary –

RANI: But they are the powerless just trying to find a place in this
rotten society for themselves!

(RAFI *moves slowly. He is tired and distressed, but there is great
dignity in his actions. He takes the sheets from the bed and starts,
almost experimentally, to tie them together securely. The voices
outside get louder.*)

ALICE: (*Out of shot*) Their place can only be found on society's
terms, not on their own whim –

(*Cut to:* SAMMY *has come into the flat. He stands there a while,
looking at everyone.*)

ROSIE: (*To* ALICE) It's hardly whim, they have no given place in
this society!

(SAMMY *goes to* ANNA *and touches her lightly. She doesn't ignore
him, but it's as if she doesn't notice him. He looks at* ROSIE.
Cut to: Back in the study RAFI *has proceeded quite far with the
joining together of the sheets. He climbs the ladder and ties the
sheet to the top rung. Finally we see him put the other end of the
sheet around his neck. During this, he is breathing deeply. He
seems very alert now and aware of everything.
Cut to:* SAMMY *leans over* ROSIE.)

SAMMY: Where's my dad?

ROSIE: He's in his room. You OK?

(*Now we hear* RAFI *kill himself as he jumps from the ladder.*)

SAMMY: (*To* ROSIE) Sure.

(SAMMY *goes to Rafi's room. He sees his father hanging. He
looks at him.* SAMMY *leaves the study and goes back into the
living room. He watches the women talking for a moment.*)
(*To* ROSIE) Rosie, I think there's something you should come
and look at.

(*She looks up and goes to* SAMMY. *They go into the study. We see*
SAMMY *and* ROSIE *in the study looking at* RAFI.)

57

94. INT. SAMMY'S AND ROSIE'S LIVING ROOM. DAY
SAMMY *and* ROSIE *sit on the floor together, rocking each other, waiting for the ambulance. We can see the others leaving, solemnly, one by one,* ANNA *turning back to look at* SAMMY *as she goes. But he doesn't see her. It is just the two of them together.*

SOME TIME WITH STEPHEN
A Diary

2 JUNE 1986

I shove the first draft of *Sammy and Rosie Get Laid* through Stephen Frears's letterbox and run, not wanting him to see me. A few hours later he rings and says: 'This isn't an innocent act!' and refuses to read it. He says he's going to Seattle with Daniel Day Lewis for the weekend to attend a film festival and he'll read it on the plane.

I have many doubts about the script and in lots of ways it's rough, but I can't get any further with it at the moment. In fact, I can't even bear to look at it.

9 JUNE 1986

Scared of ringing Frears and asking his opinion on the script, I ring Dan and ask about the Seattle trip. I also ask – and I am shaky here – if he managed to glance at the script himself, if he perhaps had a few moments in which to pass his eyes over it. He says firmly that he did read it. I ask if Frears liked it. He says Frears did like it. Finally I ring Frears and after much small talk about cricket he says: 'I know why you've rung and it's very good!' It begins then.

10 JUNE 1986

I see the great Indian actor Shashi Kapoor on TV, on the balcony of the Indian dressing-room at the Test Match. I'd like him to play the lead in the film, the politician. I've had him in mind since Frears met him in India and said how interesting he was. We try to track him down, but by the time we get to him he's left the country.

12 JUNE 1986

Frears rings me to talk about his availability. He's not going to be around for a while, being preoccupied with *Prick Up Your Ears* and then a film he's shooting in India. I wonder if this is a subtle way of his saying he doesn't want to direct the film.

Meanwhile I send the script to Karin Bamborough at Channel 4. She and David Rose commissioned and paid for all of *My Beautiful Laundrette*. Then I ring Tim Bevan and tell him what's going on.

Bevan is a tall, hard-working man in his mid-twenties, in love with making films and doing deals. He and his partner Sarah

Radclyffe are relative newcomers in films, but between them they've been involved in several recent British films: *My Beautiful Laundrette, Caravaggio, Personal Services, Elphida, Wish You Were Here* and *A World Apart*, with many more in the pipeline. Bevan has learned and developed very quickly. He's had to, moving rapidly from making pop promos to major features. His strength as a producer is his knowledge of all aspects of film-making and his ability to protect writers and directors from financial and technical problems. He's not a frustrated writer or director either. While he makes suggestions all along about the script, the direction, the actors, he ensures that everyone is working freely in their own area; his views are valuable and informed, but he never attempts to impose them.

He's keen to read the script and thinks that after the success of the *Laundrette* in the US it shouldn't be a problem raising some of the money there. But Frears won't give Bevan a script to read because Bevan's going to LA and Frears doesn't want him to try and raise money for it. Frears is still working out how best to get the film made. He doesn't want to be pushed into doing it any particular way.

It's a relief to me that other people are involved. Getting a film going is like pushing a huge rock up the side of a mountain and until now, writing the script, I've been doing this alone. Now other people can take the weight.

13 JUNE 1986

I've known Stephen Frears since October 1984 when I sent him the first draft of *My Beautiful Laundrette*. It was made in February and March 1985 and released later that year. After its success in Britain and the US it is slowly opening around the world and Frears, Bevan, the actors and I are still promoting it in various places.

Frears is in his mid-forties and has made four feature films: *Gumshoe, The Hit, My Beautiful Laundrette* and *Prick Up Your Ears*. He's also produced and directed many films for television, where he served his apprenticeship and worked with many of the best British dramatic writers: Alan Bennett, David Hare, Stephen Poliakoff, Peter Prince, Christopher Hampton. Frears was part of the *Monty Python* generation at Cambridge, where he studied

Law; many of his contemporaries went into film, TV, theatre and journalism. Later he worked at the Royal Court Theatre as an assistant to Lindsay Anderson.

Whatever Frears wears, he always looks as if he's slept in his clothes and his hair just stands straight up on the top and shoots out at the sides as if he's been electrocuted. His idea of dressing up is to put on a clean pair of plimsolls. The sartorial message is: I can't think about all that stuff, it means nothing to me, I'm a bohemian not a fashion slave. When we were shooting the *Laundrette* Daniel Day Lewis would go up to Stephen as if Stephen were a tramp, and press 20p in his hand, saying: 'Please accept this on behalf of the Salvation Army and buy yourself a cup of tea!'

I was drawn to him from the start because of his irreverence and seriousness, his directness and kindness. While he hates words like 'artist' and 'integrity', since they smack of self-regard, he is immensely skilled and talented; and though he talks a lot about how much money certain directors make, he never makes a film entirely for the money. He has great interest and respect for the young, for their music and films and political interests. As his own generation settles down into comfort and respectability, he is becoming more adventurous and disrespectful of British society, seeing it as part of his work to be sceptical, questioning, doubting and polemical.

Frears's nonconformity and singularity, his penchant for disruption and anarchy, suit and inform the area of film we inhabit, an area which has been especially exciting recently, that of low-budget films made quickly and sometimes quite roughly; films made, to a certain extent, outside the system of studios and big film companies, films that the people involved in can control themselves.

The freshness of these films has been due partly to the subject matter, the exploration of areas of British life not touched on before. Just as one of the excitements of British culture in the sixties was the discovery of the lower middle class and working class as a subject, one plus of the repressive eighties has been cultural interest in marginalized and excluded groups.

So I ring Frears and give him an earful about why I think he should direct *Sammy and Rosie Get Laid*. I lay off the flattery for fear of making him extra suspicious, and get technical. I emphasize that it'll be a continuation of the work we've started with *Laundrette* – the mixture of realism and surrealism, seriousness and comedy, art and gratuitous sex.

Frears listens to all this patiently. Then he suddenly says we should make the film for television, on 16mm. I quickly say that I'm not convinced by that. He argues that the equipment is much lighter; you can make films faster. So he suggests we give it to the BBC. If they like it, he says they'll pay for it and our problems will be over. I counter by saying they've become too reactionary, terrified of ripe language and screwing, cowed by censors. If you want to show an arse on the BBC, they behave as if their entire licence fee were at stake.

All the same, he says finally, he sees it as a TV thing, done in the spirit of *Laundrette*.

I watch scenes on TV of South African police beating up protestors and wonder what the minds of the cops must be like. That's partly what I want to get at with *Sammy and Rosie* – it's my puzzling about the mind of a torturer, the character of a man capable of extreme violence and cruelty while he continues to live a life with others. Does he speak of love in the evenings?

Receive a letter from an aunt who lives in the north of England. After seeing *Laundrette* she frequently rings my father to abuse him. 'Your son is a complete bastard!' she screeches down the phone, as if it's my father's fault I write such things. 'Can't you control the little bastard!' she yells. 'Humiliating us in public! Suppose people find out I'm related to him!'

In her letter she says: 'I tried to phone you, but I believe you were in the USA boring the pants off the Americans with your pornography . . . Worst of all, the film was offensive to your father's distinguished family. Uncle was portrayed in a very bad light, drunk in bed with his brand of vodka, and uncut toenails . . . this was totally uncalled for and mischievous. It only brings to light your complete lack of loyalty, integrity and compassion . . . We didn't know you were a "poofter". We do hope you're aware of AIDS and its dangers, if not, then a medical leaflet can be sent to you. Why oh why do you have to promote the widely held view of the British that all evil stems from Pakistani immigrants? Thank goodness for top quality films like *Gandhi*.'

64

I think of something Thackeray wrote in *Vanity Fair:* 'If a man has committed wrong in life, I don't know any moralist more anxious to point his errors out to the world than his own relations.'

I decide to name the Asian lesbian in *Sammy and Rosie* after her.

Earlier this year I ran into Philip Roth at a party and told him about the hostility I'd received from this aunt and other Pakistanis complaining about their portrayal in *Laundrette* and other things I'd written. Roth said the same thing happened to him after *Portnoy's Complaint.* Indeed he writes about this in *The Ghost Writer.*

In that novel, Nathan, a young Jewish novelist 'looking for admiration and praise', writes a story about an old family feud. He shows it to his father. The father is shattered by the public betrayal. 'You didn't leave anything out,' he moans. Except the achievements, the hard work, the decency. He adds sadly: 'I wonder if you fully understand just how little love there is in this world for Jewish people.'

When Nathan protests that they are in Newark, not Germany, father seeks a second opinion, that of Judge Leopold Wapter. Wapter immediately applies the literary acid test which he believes every Jewish book must endure: will the story warm the heart of Joseph Goebbels? The result is . . . positive. So why, why, screams Wapter, in a story with a Jewish background, must there be adultery, incessant fighting within a family over money and warped human behaviour in general?

What Wapter's Complaint demands is 'positive images'. It requires useful lies and cheering fictions: the writer as public relations officer, as hired liar.

Like *Laundrette, Sammy and Rosie* is quite a personal story, autobiographical, not in its facts, but emotionally. The woman involved (I'll call her Sarah) asked to read the script. I said no, because the character will change as the film goes through several drafts; the actress playing the part will also change it, as will Frears when he starts to work on it. It's also difficult to write accurately about real people in fiction – however much you might want to – because the demands of the idea are usually such that you have to transform the original person to fit the constraints of the story. All the same, I'm nervous about what Sarah will think of it. I know that in certain passages I've been spiteful.

On the phone Frears talks about Art Malik for the part of Sammy. He's an attractive actor, but we both wonder if he's fly enough for the role.

20 JUNE 1986
Meeting at Channel 4 with Karin Bamborough and David Rose to discuss the film. Together they've been the architects of a remarkable number of low-budget independent films which are mostly (or partly) funded by TV money for theatrical release. This series of films has ensured a revival in British film-making (they're almost the only people making films in Britain today) and has given encouragement to women and black film-makers, first-time directors and writers, working on material that wouldn't be acceptable to the mainstream commercial world.

Their success has partly been due to their initiative in approaching writers from other forms – novelists, playwrights, short-story writers and journalists – to write films. They know that usually the best screenplays are not written by people who call themselves screenwriters, but by good writers, writers who excel in other forms. After all, the 'rules' of screenwriting can be learned in an hour. But the substance of a decent screenplay, character, story, mood, pace, can only come from a cultivated imagination. Although it's virtually impossible to make a good film without a good screenplay, screenwriting itself is such a bastardized, ignoble profession (director Joseph Mankiewicz said 'the screenwriter is the highest-paid secretary in the world') that writers who wish to survive, have to avoid it, turning only to the movies as a well-paid sideline, regrettably not regarding it as a serious medium.

Karin tells me that the characters in the first draft aren't strong enough yet. I'll have to do two or three more drafts. David Rose says he regrets it all being set in London since he feels too many C4 films have been set there. Can't I set it in Birmingham, he says.

21 JUNE 1986
The contract arrives from C4 offering a commission for *Sammy and Rosie*. They're offering a pathetic amount of money.

66

6 JULY 1986

My agent rings me in New York to say the idea now is to form a three-way company to make the film: Frears, Bevan and Sarah Radclyffe, and I. This way we'll be able to control everything about the film.

9 JULY 1986

I speak to Frears who is about to start filming *Prick Up Your Ears*. He says he wants to prepare *Sammy and Rosie* after he's finished his Indian film. This means we'll shoot it in the autumn of 1987. It's a long time to wait: I feel let down, life goes slack once more. But it'll force me to write something else in the meantime.

9 AUGUST 1986

Lunch at '192' in Notting Hill with Bevan and Radclyffe, and Frears. Shashi arrives with his secretary after everyone else. He has on a loose brown costume, with a dark red and chocolate scarf flung over his shoulder. He is so regal and dignified, stylish and exotic, that a shiver goes through the restaurant.

I mention that though this is the first time we've met, I saw him on the balcony at the Lord's Test. He says he wore the same clothes then and had trouble getting into the pavilion, so conventional and uptight are the MCC. So he told them he'd just had lunch with Mrs Thatcher and if his national dress was good enough for the Prime Minister surely it would be acceptable to the MCC.

In the charm department he has real class and yet he is genuinely modest. I feel a little embarrassed at asking him to be in this film, small and fairly sordid as it is. But Shashi says he thinks the script is better than that for *Laundrette*. He adds that he's available at our convenience.

It's a sunny day and when Shashi leaves we stroll back to Frears's house, pleased with Shashi's enthusiasm. We talk a bit about the other parts: Claire Bloom as Alice, with Miranda Richardson or Judy Davis as Rosie perhaps.

Frears talks about the part of Anna, the American photographer, saying she isn't sympathetic enough: I've parodied her. He's right about this and I lack grip on the character. The process of writing is so much one of seeking ideas in one's unconscious, whatever they are, and then later justifying them, filling them out and finding what the hell they mean, if anything. The entire script will have to be subject to this scrutiny.

At last I give the script to Sarah to read. Sarah and I met at university and lived together for six years. Since she moved out, we've continued to see a lot of each other.

When Sarah reads it she is angry and upset at the same time. I've said things that she feels are true, but which I've never said to her. The worry is, she adds, that people will think she is Rosie and she'll be petrified like that for ever, with her freedom possessed by the camera. She'll no longer be in reasonable control of the way people think of her. Won't they have this crude cinema idea?

All this makes me feel guilty and sneaky; it makes me think that writers are like spies, poking into failures and weaknesses for good stories. Necessarily, because that's how they see the world, writers constantly investigate the lives of the people they are involved with. They keep private records of these private relationships. And on the surface they appear to be participating normally in life. But a few years later, it's all written down, embellished, transformed, distorted, but still a recognizable bit of someone's lived life.

Bevan has sent the script to Art Malik and Miranda Richardson, who I ran into the other day at the Royal Court. I told her about the film and she seemed interested, but it seems she'll be doing the Spielberg film *Empire of the Sun* at the same time.

To Paris with Frears, Bevan and Daniel Day Lewis. Everywhere you go here British films are showing: *Clockwise*, *Mona Lisa*, *Room with a View*, *Laundrette*. There seem to be more cinemas per square kilometre here than anywhere else I've been. I do interviews all day through an interpreter who is the daughter-in-law of Raymond Queneau.

Dan is something of a star now, and as an actor has moved on to another plane. He's here rehearsing for the movie of *The Unbear-*

able Lightness of Being. Dan dresses in black and doesn't shave. He carries a black bag hooped across his body and looks like an artist, a painter, as he strides across bridges and down boulevards.

We meet to chat in the bar of the George V Hotel where Frears is being interviewed. The journalist says admiringly to Frears: 'I've met a lot of men like you, only they're all Italian.'

Frears has thought a great deal about how to do *Sammy and Rosie* and has now decided that the best thing is to make it on 35mm for theatrical release, keeping the budget as low as possible. Bevan thinks we can raise most of the money for the film in America. Frears thinks this is a good idea since it'll save Channel 4 money: they'll be able to give the money to film-makers who can't get money elsewhere.

18 DECEMBER 1986

Suddenly we're going into production at the beginning of January, shooting early in March, as Frears's Indian project has been delayed. So the script has to start looking ready. Try to get the story going earlier, Frears says. And the riots: we're too familiar with them from television. Something more has to be going on than people throwing bottles at policemen. I interpret this to mean that what happens between the characters during these scenes is of primary interest.

I meet Frances Barber in the production office. She's a very experienced theatre actor and I've known her work for years, as she's risen up through the fringe to join the RSC. She's done some film work (she was in *Prick Up Your Ears*), but not yet played a major role. The feeling is that she's ready, that she's at the stage Daniel was at just before *Laundrette*. She talks well about the script and can see the problems of playing against characters with the charm I've tried to give Rafi, and the bright childishness of Sammy. Rosie mustn't seem moralistic or self-righteous.

Later Frears rings me, delighted to be in the middle of an interview with a young Pakistani actor, Ayub Khan Din, who is upstairs having a pee and is being considered for the part of Sammy. Art Malik, who we discussed first but were sceptical of, has anyway complained about the scenes in bed with Anna and about the scene where Sammy wanks, snorts coke and sucks on a milkshake at the same time. In the end he says the script isn't good enough. I think he prefers easier and more glamorous kinds of roles.

Ayub had a small part in *Laundrette* which was later cut from the film. I remember him coming to the cast screening, eager to see himself in his first film, and Frears having to take him to one side to explain that, well, unfortunately, he'd had to cut his big scene. Since then Ayub has grown and developed, though he's only twenty-five and the part was written for someone older.

Now the film is going ahead and other people are starting to get involved, I can feel my responsibility for it diminishing. This is a relief to me. I've done most of the hard work I have to do. Now I can enjoy the process of the film being shot and released. Any rewriting I do from now on will be nothing compared with the isolated and unhelped strain of working out the idea in the first place.

I remember sitting in a hotel room in Washington, overlooking the Dupont Circle, drinking beer after beer and trying to jump over the high wall which was the halfway point of the script. I got stuck for months with the film after the 'fuck' night – the climax, the section at the centre where the three couples copulate simultaneously. (Originally I wanted to call the film *The Fuck*.) What would be the consequences of these three acts? What would they mean to all the characters and how would these acts change them? It wasn't until I decided to extend the waste ground material and the consequent eviction, until I introduced this new element, that I was able to continue. The problem was whether this material would be convincing. It wasn't based on anything I'd known, though for a long time I've been interested in anarchist ideas – a respectable English political tradition, from Winstanley, through William Godwin and onwards. If anything, it was based on some of the young people who'd attended theatre workshops I'd given. They had terrific energy, intelligence and inventiveness. But because of poverty, homelessness, unemployment and bad schooling, they were living in the interstices of the society: staying in squats, dealing drugs, and generally scavenging around. It seemed to me that this society had little to offer them, no idea how to use them or what to do with their potential.

Because of this block I frequently thought of abandoning the film. I wrote the same scene twenty-five or thirty times in the hope of a breakthrough. I'd set up this complicated story; I'd invented the characters and let things happen between them, but then it all stopped. This is where real life or direct autobiography fails you: the story has to be completed on its own terms.

Sarah Radclyffe has some reservations about the script. She doubts whether Sammy and Rosie would be ignorant of Rafi's involvement in the torture of his political enemies, especially if they'd been to visit him in his own country. Karin Bamborough said something similar and suggested I change it so the film opened with them all meeting for the first time. That would be a considerable rewrite. Also, there's no reason why they should have found out about the details of Rafi's crimes since he would have worked through hired hit-men and through people who wouldn't necessarily have been immediately identified with him. It would have taken years for this information to be discovered and collated.

This morning in our office it was like the Royal Court in exile. Frears, myself, and Debbie McWilliams (the casting director) all worked at the Court. Tunde Ikoli, a young writer and director who worked as Lindsay Anderson's assistant at the Court, was in the office. We see a number of interesting and experienced black actors. Things have certainly changed in that respect from four or five years ago. Many of these actors who have either worked at the National Theatre's Studio with Peter Gill (ex-Royal Court) or at the Court serve to remind us of the importance of the theatre, not only in itself, but as a seedbed for film and TV.

We talk about the audience there is for our kind of films. Aged between eighteen and forty, mostly middle class and well-educated, film- and theatre-literate, liberal progressive or leftish, this massive and sophisticated audience doesn't want to be patronized by teen films: they'll support a poor and rough cinema rich in ideas and imagination.

21 DECEMBER 1986

Michael Barker from Orion Classics rings to say Orion are going to push for an Oscar nomination for me. He doesn't think I'll

71

win – Woody Allen will win for *Hannah and Her Sisters* – but he thinks he can swing the nomination.

23 DECEMBER 1986

Hugo, the film's designer, rings to say they've found an excellent location for the caravan site. This is in Notting Hill. The flat concrete curve of the motorway hangs above a dusty stretch of waste ground which itself is skirted by a mainline railway line and a tube track. I know the area he means and it's excellent.

They're also looking for a house in the area to serve as Sammy's and Rosie's flat. There's been talk of building it in a studio which would be easier, but Frears feels at the moment it should be done on location.

Bevan is trying to find an area where we can stage the riots. There are obviously problems with the police over this, and I'll have to prepare a doctored script to show them. When he goes to see them he refers to the riots as 'scuffles'!

I run into Claire Bloom in the street nearby and yesterday I met her husband, Philip Roth, in a health-food shop in Notting Hill. He asks how the film is going and tells me he prefers to keep away from films, not having liked any of the films made from his books. It reminds me of the second time I met Philip and Claire. Frears and I were outside the American Embassy walking through the crowd protesting against the bombing of Libya. Mostly the occasion was like a Methodist church fête. Then, there at the barrier nearest to the Embassy were Philip and Claire, very angry.

24 DECEMBER 1986

Frears and I talk about *Sammy and Rosie* in its style and rhythm, being far more leisurely than *Laundrette*. The relationships are more developed; it needs more room to breathe. It's less of a shocker; more of a grown-up film.

29 DECEMBER 1986

Frears slightly miffed by the realization of how much Thatcher would approve of us: we're a thrifty, enterprising, money-making small business. I say: But part of our purpose is to make popular films which are critical of British society. He says: Thatcher wouldn't care about that, she'd just praise our initiative for doing something decent despite the odds; the real difficulty of making films in Britain today made more difficult by this government.

4 JANUARY 1987
Long meeting with Frears last night at his house. The first time, really, we've sat down and discussed the script. His ideas are exactly the stimulation I've been waiting for to enable me to find a resolution to the film. After the 'fuck' night the film fragments, the intercutting is too quick, the scenes are too short. This is because I haven't worked out exactly what is going on, what I want to say. What Frears and I do, as we talk, as he puts his children to bed, is invent new elements to bind the story together: Rani and Vivia putting pressure on Rafi; Rani and Vivia putting pressure on Rosie with regard to Rafi living in her flat; some of the other women pursuing Rafi through the city, perhaps harrying him to his death; all the characters (and not just some of them, as it is now) meeting at the eviction scene and their relationships being resolved there.

Now I have to sit down and look at the whole thing again. It's not as if I can rewrite bits and pieces. It'll be an entirely new draft. I suppose if you want to be a decent writer you have to have the ability to rip up what you've done and go back and start again, tear up your best lines and ideas and replace them with better lines and ideas, however hard this is and however long it takes.

5 JANUARY 1987
I get up at six in the morning unable to sleep so paranoid am I about this thing ever getting rewritten. In this frozen deserted city I start to fiddle with the script, contra what I said yesterday. When I realize the futility of this fiddling I put a fresh sheet in the typewriter and start at page 1. I do no planning, give it no thought and just go at it, walking out on the tightrope. The idea is not to inhibit myself, not be over-critical or self-conscious or self-censoring, otherwise I'll get blocked and the act of writing will be like trying to drive a car with the brakes on.

Today is the first day of pre-production and everyone officially starts work: the director, the casting director, the production manager, designer and so on. The young lighting cameraman,

Oliver Stapleton, is going to shoot this film, as he did *Laundrette*. That film was his first feature, though since then he's done *Absolute Beginners* and *Prick Up Your Ears*. So it's all terrifically exciting. What a shame that it feels as if the script is disintegrating in my hands. The new ideas touch every other element in the film, altering them, giving them different significance. Little of what I've written seems secure now, except the characters; certainly not the story. As the whole thing goes into the mixer my fear is that it'll all fall apart.

7 JANUARY 1987

I write a scene this morning between Rani, Vivia and Rosie at the end of the party, which is crucial to the film. Rani and Vivia accuse Rosie of lacking political integrity. It's a dramatic scene and will wind the film up just when it needs it. I'm surprised that it's taken me so long to see how useful this kind of pressure on Rosie could be. It's partly because it's only since that conversation with Frears that I've seen the point of Rani and Vivia in the film. They were in the first draft – I dropped them in because unconsciously I knew they'd be of use. It's taken me till the fourth draft to find out for what exactly.

8 JANUARY 1987

I spend most of the day trying to write a final scene for the film, which at the moment is Rafi staggering around on the waste ground during the eviction, and Sammy standing on the motorway shouting down at Rosie without being heard. This isn't satisfactory. So I try going back to a previous ending, which has Rosie and Margy and Eva, her women friends, deciding to move into the flat with Rosie while Sammy goes off on his own to a house he's bought. But I don't believe in this ending.

Usually when I have a block I put the film or story in a drawer for thirty days, like putting a pie in the oven, and when I take it out it's cooked. But there isn't time for that now.

So I put the last few pages in the typewriter and rewrite them, trying to quieten my mind and allow fresh ideas to pop in as they will. So it occurs to me, or rather it writes itself, that Rafi should hang himself. As the words go down I know I'm on to something dramatic and powerful. I'm also doing something which will be depressing. I've no idea how this suicide will affect the rest of the film and no idea what it means or says. I can work that out later. It's a relief to have had a new idea, and a creative pleasure to solve a problem not by refining what one has already done, but to slam down a bizarre and striking fresh image!

10 JANUARY 1987
Bevan, Rebecca (the location manager), Jane (production manager) and I go to North Kensington to look at locations for the scenes at the beginning of the film with Rosie visiting the old man and finding him dead in the bath, waiting for the ambulance, and watching the boys' bonfire in the centre of the estate. To the thirtieth floor of a tower block (which won design awards in the sixties), with several young kids in the lift. The lift is an odd shape: very deep, with a low roof. Jane says this is so they can get bodies in coffins down from the thirtieth floor. We walk around other blocks in the area. They are filthy, derelict places, falling down, graffiti-sprayed, wind-blown, grim and humming with the smell of shit, implacable in the hatred of humanity they embody. The surrounding shops are barricaded with bars and wire mesh. I was brought up in London. It's my city. I'm no Britisher, but a Londoner. And it's filthier and more run down now than it's ever been.

I get home and speak to Frears on the phone. The double imperative: that the rewritten script be handed in on Monday and yet, as he says, be more intricate. 'Deeper' is the word he uses. Christ. Have told no one yet about the new ending.

I have the sense today of the film starting to move away from me, of this little thing which I wrote in my bedroom in Fulham now becoming public property. On the crew list there are now already fifty names, at least a quarter of them from *Laundrette*.

12 JANUARY 1987
Frears comes over. I sit opposite him as he turns over the pages of the script. We talk about each page. Because the film is about the relations between men and women in contemporary Britain and has political content, we're beginning to realize how important it is that it says what we want it to say. That means working out what it is we believe!

As Frears gets nearer the end I get more nervous. I've typed up the scene where Rafi hangs himself and it's quite different from the innocuous and rather dissipated finales so far.

After reading it Frears says nothing for a while. He jumps up and walks round and round the flat. It's started to snow outside; it's very cold. Is he just trying to keep warm?

We talk until 1.30 about this end and worry whether it's too brutal both on the audience and as an act of aggression by Rafi against the rest of the characters he's become involved with. We talk about the possibility of Rafi dying of a heart attack! But this is too contingent. It's the power of the deliberate act that we like.

We discuss Chekhov's *Seagull*. I say Rafi's suicide could be like Trepliov's at the end of that play: understated, with the action off-stage, one person discovering it and then returning to the room to tell everyone else. In this room there'd be: Rani, Vivia, Alice, Anna, Eva, Bridget, Rosie.

We decide to leave it for the moment. More importantly, we're going to New York soon to cast Anna the photographer. I'm still not clear what she's doing in the film. I've deliberately avoided rewriting her bits.

13 JANUARY 1987
Seven in the morning and freezing cold. Streets covered in snow. Behind me I can hear the tubes rattling along at the back of the house. Outside the careful traffic and people starting to go to work. I'm not in the mood for rewriting this thing. Still a few scenes to be revised, but I'm sick of it. It says on the piece of paper in front of me: fifth draft, but in reality it must be the eighth or ninth. If each draft is about 100 pages, that's 900 pages of writing!

When I first moved into this part of West London, in 1978, I felt vulnerable. It was like living on the street. People walked by on their way to work just yards from my head. In time I relaxed and would lie in bed and hear and feel London around me, stretching out for miles.

These West London streets by the railway line have gone wrong. In 1978 most of the five-storey houses with their crumbling pillars, peeling façades and busted windows were derelict, inhabited by itinerants, immigrants, drug-heads and people not ashamed of being seen drunk on the street. On the balcony opposite a man regularly practised the bagpipes at midnight. Now the street is crammed with people who work for a living. Young men wear striped shirts and striped ties; the women wear blue jumpers with white shirts, turned-up collars and noses, and pearls. They drive Renault 5s and late at night as you walk along the street, you can see them in their clean shameless basements having dinner parties and playing Trivial Pursuits on white tablecloths. Now the centre of the city is inhabited by the young rich and serviced by everyone else: now there is the re-establishment of firm class divisions; now the sixties and the ideals of that time seem like an impossible dream or naivety.

Though I was at school and not politically active in 1968, I was obsessively aware of the excitement and originality of those years. I had the records, the books, the clothes; I saw the sixties on TV and was formed by what I missed out on. I wasn't involved enough to become disillusioned. The attitudes that formed me are, briefly: that openness and choice in sexual behaviour is liberating and that numerous accretions of sexual guilt and inhibi-tion are psychologically damaging; that the young are innately original and vigorous, though this special quality is to do with not being burdened with responsibility and the determinations of self-interest; that there should be a fluid, non-hierarchical society with free movement across classes and that these classes will eventually be dissolved; that ambition and competitiveness are stifling narrowers of personality; and that all authority should be viewed with suspicion and constantly questioned.

The past ten years of repression have been a continuous sur-prise to me. Somehow I haven't been able to take them seriously, since I imagine the desire for more freedom, more pleasure, more self-expression to be fundamental to life. So I continue to think, in that now old way, in terms of the 'straight' world and the rest, the more innocent and lively ones standing against the corrupt and stuffy. I still think of businessmen as semi-criminals; I'm suspicious of anyone in a suit; I like drugs, especially hash, and I can't understand why people bother to get married. Ha!

14 JANUARY 1987
Frears rings and says the scene where Alice tells Rafi to go, at the

end of the film after he's been chased out of Sammy's and Rosie's flat by Vivia and Rani, is boring, boring, boring. There has to be a dramatic action rather than extended verbals as it is now. I say: well what fucking dramatic action? He says: no idea – you do the paperwork, I just do the pictures!

16 JANUARY 1987
Frances Barber seems enthusiastic about the rewrites but says she'd been disturbed by the new end. It reverses the film, she thinks, in that Rafi now seems to accept his guilt for torturing people. Frances says this seems inconsistent with his having argued so strongly for political expediency in the restaurant scene. I say I don't want him committing suicide out of guilt. It's that he's come to the end. No one wants him. There's nowhere for him to go, neither at home nor in Britain.

Frears has a session with Frances and Ayub, which he videotapes. Ayub is very nervous, not surprisingly. We've cast Frances and probably Ayub will be offered the part tomorrow.

17 JANUARY 1987
We look at the tape of Frances and Ayub together. They look good together. Ayub waits downstairs in his agent's office, refusing to go home until we make our decision. He comes into the room looking dazed with tension. We offer him the job. He thanks us all and shakes hands with us.

Frears has decided that the film should be much more about young people than I'd imagined. Because of Ayub being five years younger than Frances we could as easily cast the people around them down in age as up. Frears says casting it young will make it more cheerful. I'm all for cheerfulness, though worried that Rosie will seem oddly older than everyone else.

18 JANUARY 1987
Frears talks about the problems of shooting the riots, especially after a friend said: Oh no, not a lot of black people rioting. So we talk about avoiding the TV news-footage approach: screaming mobs, bleeding policemen. What you don't get in news footage is detail. In *The Battle of Algiers*, for example, the director humanizes the violence. You see the faces of those to whom

78

violence is being done. In the torture scene, you don't see the act, but only the faces of those around it, streaming tears.

In *Sammy and Rosie* you do see the circumstances from which the riot comes – the shooting of a black woman by the police. And we see, in the circumstances, how justifiable the riot is. The difficulty arises from the fact that black people are so rarely represented on TV; if when they are shown, they're only throwing rocks at the police, you're in danger of reinforcing considerable prejudice. I suppose this depends partly on how you see the riot, or revolt. I know I supported it, but as Orwell says about Auden, it's easy to say that if you're elsewhere when the violence takes place.

After Frears said the Alice–Rafi parting scene at the end of the film isn't dramatic enough I shake my brains and come up with a Miss Havisham scene set in the cellar of the house. I have Alice furiously throwing open a suitcase in which she's packed the clothes she'd intended to take on her planned elopement with Rafi in the mid-fifties. I also have her showing Rafi the diaries she kept then, in which she poured out her heart to him – the physical and visual representation of what was formerly just dialogue.

To the opera on Friday with a vegetarian friend. A woman in a long sable coat sits next to us. My friend says: I wish I carried a can of spray paint in my bag and could shoot it over her coat. Thought it might be an idea to stick in the film. But where?

20 JANUARY 1987
Debbie McWilliams saw a pop group, the Fine Young Cannibals, on TV and asks the singer, Roland Gift, to come into the office. He shows up looking splendid, proud and vulnerable, with his manager. I ask the women in the office to get a look at him through the office window and let us know if they want to rip his clothes off with their teeth. As most of them seem to want this, Roland inches closer to the part of Danny.

On the way home from the movies the other night, at Piccadilly tube station a group of young Jewish kids gathers at the top of the escalator. Suddenly, around them, are a bunch of Arsenal football supporters who stand and chant 'Yiddo, yiddo!' at these kids. The kids look embarrassed rather than frightened, but they do move closer together, standing in a little huddle. It's a difficult

moment. What do you do when it comes to it? Walk on, watch, or
pile in? What are you made of? What would you give up? I can
see a lot of other dithering people in the vicinity have this
dilemma. But no one does anything. The chanting goes on. Then
the youths disappear down the escalator, their voices echoing
around the building. It's the first time I've seen this kind of
anti-Semitism in London. Decide to put it in the film somewhere.
The structure is secure enough now for anything odd or interesting that happens to have a place. All the bits and pieces will just
have to get along with each other, like people at a party.

23 JANUARY 1987
Problems with Meera Syal, the actress we want to play Rani. Max
Stafford-Clark, artistic director of the Royal Court, rings to say
Meera has already committed herself to Caryl Churchill's play
Serious Money. She also wants to play Rani in our film. At the
moment the schedule can't be arranged so she can do both. We
don't want to press her to choose, for fear she'll choose the Court.
It's painful to her, especially as Asian actors get offered so little
work.

Anyway, we'll deal with it later. In the meantime we're going to
my favourite city, New York!

25 JANUARY 1987
New York. This city is snowbound and every time you look
round, someone has skidded on to their back in the street. New
York is cold in a way London never is: here your face freezes,
here the fluid in your eyes seems to ice over.

The entrance of our hotel, on Central Park West, has a silver-
lined overhang in which bright lights are embedded. This ensures
that the hotel shines like a battery of torches in a blackout for
hundreds of yards around; indeed, if you're driving through the
park you can see it glowing through the trees. In this overhang
there are heaters which warm the street and melt insubordinate
snowflakes which may drift on to the hotel's red carpet or float on
to the hat of the doorman. Everywhere you go in this city there
are notices urging you to save energy while outside this hotel they
are heating the street!

Frears is a prisoner in his hotel room, doing publicity for *Prick*

80

Up Your Ears. Food and drink is brought up to him. Between interviews he looks out of the window at Central Park. His talk schedule is exhausting. There was a time when I thought that talking about yourself to someone who said little, listened intently and made notes or recorded what you said was the ideal relationship. But after the first three hours your tongue is dry, your mouth will not work, your jaws ache, as after six hours of fellatio. The only respite is to question the journalists and hope they'll revive you by telling you about themselves.

A journalist asks me how I came upon the central idea of *Sammy and Rosie*. I start to think about it, but it is complicated; an idea usually has many sources.

One source was the great Japanese film *Tokyo Story* in which an old couple who live in the country go to visit their children in the city and are treated shabbily by them. I started off thinking of *Sammy and Rosie* as a contemporary remake of this desperately moving and truthful film. Sometimes I wish my own script had the simplicity, luminosity and straightforward humanity of Ozu's masterpiece, that I hadn't added so many characters, themes and gewgaws.

Another source was a play I once wrote and abandoned about an Asian politician living in London in the sixties and having an affair with a young woman. I retained the politician and dropped everything else.

There was also a story I was told about a member of my family who loved an Englishwoman, left her after promising to return to England to marry her, and never came back, though the word is she loves him still and continues to wait.

When Frears has finished his interviews for the day he says a journalist told him, when they were discussing British films, that he didn't think anything dramatic ever happened in Britain now. This journalist's view of Britain sounds like Orson Welles in *The Third Man* talking about Switzerland, only capable of producing the cuckoo clock!

The journalist's remark hits a nerve. It relates to the British sense of inferiority about its film industry: not only the feeling that the British can't really make good films, but that contemporary British subjects and themes are really too small, too insignificant as subjects. So British films are often aimed at American audiences and attempt to deal with 'universal' or 'epic' themes as in *Gandhi*, *The Mission*, *The Killing Fields*, *Cry Freedom*.

The journalist's view isn't entirely surprising since a lot of English 'art' also dwells, gloats on and relives nostalgic scenarios of wealth and superiority. It's easy therefore for Americans to see Britain as just an old country, as a kind of museum, as a factory for producing versions of lost greatness. After all, many British films do reflect this: *Chariots of Fire*, *A Room with a View*, the Raj epics, and the serials *Brideshead Revisited* and *The Jewel in the Crown*. Even the recent past, the Beatles, punks, the numerous Royal Weddings, are converted into quaintness, into tourist mugs and postcards, into saleable myths. If imperialism is the highest form of capitalism, then tourism is its ghostly afterlife in this form of commercial nostalgia which is sold as 'art' or 'culture'.

But some British dignity remains, unlike in New York where a friend of mine rings a fashionable restaurant on a Saturday night and they tell him they don't have a table. My friend, who in the American manner is very persistent, says he is bringing a screenwriter with him – me. The person in the restaurant asks: We may be able to squeeze your party in, sir, but please tell me: what are the screenwriter's credits?!

26 JANUARY 1987
We troop off to the famous theatrical restaurant Sardi's for an award dinner. Like executioners, photographers in black balaclavas crowd the entrance. Going in, I realize we've arrived too early. We sit down and they bring us our food while others are still arriving. The salmon tastes like wallpaper. Around the walls there are hideous caricatures of film stars and famous writers. Thankfully the ceremony is not televised or competitive: you know if you've won; they don't torment you with any opening of envelopes. Sissy Spacek and Lynn Redgrave, obviously experienced at the awards game, time it just right, so that when they arrive the whole room is in place and is forced to turn and look at them. Photographers shove through the crowd and climb across tables to get to them.

I see Norman Mailer come in. He is stocky like a boxer and healthy of face, though he looks frail when he walks. It will be a thrilling moment for me to have the great man rest his eyes on me when I receive my award for the *Laundrette* screenplay. When the playwright Beth Henley announces my name I eagerly look out for Mailer from the podium. I start into my speech but almost stop talking when I see Mailer's place is now vacant and across the restaurant he is rapidly mounting the stairs to watch the final of the Super Bowl on TV.

27 JANUARY 1987

Spend two mornings in the hotel room interviewing actresses for the part of Anna. About twenty come in and we have longish conversations with all of them: they're frank and lively and seem healthier and more confident than their British counterparts, somehow less beaten down by things. They are less educated too. The American film world isn't adjacent to the theatre or literary world as it can be in London. It's closer to rock 'n' roll, if anything.

An actress called Wendy Gazelle seems untypical of the group we see. She is less forthright, more sensitive and attractive in a less orthodox way. When Wendy reads, in that room overlooking the park through which people are skiing, it is heartbreaking. I'm so pleased she can invest the somewhat duff dialogue with feeling and meaning that I urge the others to choose her.

In the evening to the Café Luxembourg with Leon from Cinecom, the company that, along with Channel 4, is financing our film. Frears and I refer to Leon as 'the man that owns us', which he doesn't seem to mind. He's thirty-four, friendly and intelligent, with long hair in a pigtail. Bevan, Frears and I are apprehensive about the pressure his company might put on us to massage or roll our film in a certain direction. We'll just have to wait and see.

28 JANUARY 1987

To a smart party on the Upper West Side, given by a New York agent for the German director Doris Dorrie. It's a large apartment in front of which is a courtyard and behind it a view of the river. Marcie, the publicist for *Laundrette* in New York says: I wouldn't object to being the accountant of the people in this room! She points out: Isabella Rossellini, Alan Pakula, Matthew Modine, Michael Douglas and various others. Michael Douglas, polite and friendly, praises the British Royal Family to Frears and me for a considerable time, obviously thinking this'll please us. On the way back we pass a laundromat called *My Beautiful Laundrette* done up in neon: it offers Reverse Cycle Washing, Fluff Drying and Expert Folding. Two days later I go back and this laundrette has closed for good.

We wonder why the film has done well in the US. It's partly, I think, because of its theme of success at any price; and partly because the puritan and prurient theme of two outcast boys (outcast from society and having escaped the world of women), clinging together in passionate blood-brotherhood is a dream of American literature and film from *Huckleberry Finn* to the work of Walt Whitman and on to *Butch Cassidy and the Sundance Kid*.

29 JANUARY 1987

I ride the subway across New York to have lunch with Leon at the Russian Tea Room. In the subway car a couple with a kid kiss shamelessly. A legless black man in a wheelchair propels himself through the car, carrying a paper cup. Everyone gives him something. The streets here are full of beggars now; every block someone asks you for money. Before going out I ensure I have a selection of loose change to give away, just as I would in Pakistan.

The young people in NY that you see on the street or subway are far less eccentric, original and fashionable than kids are in Britain. The kids in London, despite unemployment and poverty, have taste; they're adventurous and self-conscious. They're walking exhibitions: billboards of style, wearing jumble-sale and designer clothes together. In Britain fashion starts on the street. Here the kids are sartorial corpses. They all wear sports clothes. *There are even women wearing business suits and running shoes.*

The Russian Tea Room is a fashionable restaurant for movie people. It's plusher than Sardi's, apparently more 'cultured', and patronized by people who have money. It has semi-circular booths in red and gold: booths for two in the entrance, convenient for both seeing and being seen, and larger ones inside. It has a festive atmosphere. There are shining samovars, red and gold pompons on the lamp-shades and the staff wear red tunics. It's like a kind of Santa's grotto with waitresses. Powerful New York

agents do business here, reserving several booths for their clients
and associates and moving from booth to booth like door-to-door
salesmen, dealing and negotiating.

Leon has this time brought with him some serious reinforce-
ments to deal with the script 'difficulties', a beautiful and smart
woman called Shelby who works with him.

Oh, how we eat! Oh, how I like life now! I have dark brown
pancakes on which the waitress spreads sour cream. She forks a
heap of orange caviar on to this and pours liquid butter over the
lot. This is then folded. This is then placed in the mouth.

Shelby leans forward. As each caviar egg explodes on my
tongue like a little sugar bomb, Shelby tells me she has just read
all five drafts of the script. I am flattered. But more, she has
compared and contrasted them all. More wine? She talks know-
ledgeably about them. She seems to know them better than I do.
Scene 81 in draft 2, she says, is sharper than scene 79 in draft 4.
Perhaps I could go back to that? Well. I look at her. She is telling
me all this in a kindly tone. In the end, she implies, it is up to me,
but . . . She expresses her reservations, which are quite substan-
tial, at argued length.

I nod to everything, not wanting to induce indigestion. I am
also experimenting with the Zen method of bending with the
wind, so that when the cleansing storm stops, the tree of my spirit
will gaily snap back to its usual upright position. But will this
helpful puffing ever stop?

We talk about the end of the film and the hanging of Rafi. They
suggest Rafi be murdered by the Ghost. I manage to say (though I
object on principle to discussing such things at all) that this would
be predictable. Leon says: How can a Ghost murdering a politician in an anarchist commune be predictable?

By now I am sucking and licking on light ice-cream with
whipped cream and grenadine. Shelby is into her stride. Perhaps
my lack of response means I am thinking about what she is
saying? The script hasn't necessarily improved at all, it's become
cruder, more obvious. Why have you developed the black
women, Vivia and Rani? Well . . . I almost begin to fight back
when she starts to fumble in her bag. She brings out a letter.
There, read this please, she says. It's from someone who cares.

The letter, from a reader in the company, is addressed to me.

Its tone implores me to see sense. 'The version I read in October was just about perfect and the fifth draft has been tinkered with entirely too much ... The fifth draft seems a little preachy and one-dimensional. It's lost so much for the sake of clarity and it's not nearly as successful as a film ... I hope you'll consider going back to the terrific screenplay you wrote in October.'

I leave the restaurant burping on caviar and heavy with ice-cream. All afternoon I wander the city. Two dozen wasps are free within my cranium. Perhaps all those people are right. I don't know. Can't tell. God knows. My judgement has gone, swept away by the wind of all this advice. Eventually I settle down in an Irish bar – a grimy piece of Dublin – and have a few beers. I toast myself. The toast: long may you remain waterproof and never respect anyone who gives you money!

30 JANUARY 1987
Motivated entirely by greed I stay in the hotel room all day writing a 1,000-word piece about Frears for an American film magazine. They promise me $1000. On finishing it, sending it round and listening to their reservations, I realize how rarely any kind of writing is simple and how few easy bucks there are to be made. Whatever you write you always have to go back and rethink and rewrite. And you have to be prepared to do that. You never get away with anything.

5 FEBRUARY 1987
London. Good to talk to Frears again. We both say that some of the people around us have made us gloomy by expressing doubts, by emphasizing the difficulty of what we want to do. We want to work confidently, with certainty, and with pleasure. Frears is an extraordinarily cheerful man who takes great pleasure in his work and in the company of others. There's no poisonous negativity in him. It's as if he knows how close dejection and discouragement always are, that they are the converse of everything you do, and how comforting it is to let them put their arms around you.

He says this is the hardest film he's made. He said the same about *Laundrette*, and I remember feeling glad that we were doing something risky and dangerous.

10 FEBRUARY 1987

Meeting at Channel 4 with David Rose and Karin Bamborough. Karin says I'll have to give Sammy more substance as he's such a jerk and constantly making glib, flip remarks. Stephen and Tim Bevan sit chuckling at me, knowing there's some autobiography in the character. We tell Karin that Ayub is such a delightfully complicated person and so intent on playing the Oedipal relationship that he'll give the character depth. I also explain that the end will be rewritten. At the moment Rafi just hangs himself. It seems an ignoble act whereas Frears and I want it to be a justified thing, chosen, dignified, something of a Roman act.

Shashi sends his measurements in and hasn't lost any weight. We feel he's too big for the part and should look fitter and trimmer. The plan has been for Shashi to arrive a few weeks before shooting and then Bevan will shunt him off to a health farm. But so far, no sign of Shashi. Some of us are wondering whether he'll turn up at all.

As we've been concentrating on casting the other parts it now seems that Claire Bloom may not be available. A real nuisance. Fortunately the problems with Meera have been worked out and she's going to be in the film.

12 FEBRUARY 1987

I go into the production offices off Ladbroke Grove to talk about casting. There is a row of offices with glass partitions. About twenty yards away I can see Bevan waving his arms. He dashes up the corridor to tell me there's been a call from the States to say I've been nominated for an Oscar. I call my agent and she says: Goody, that'll put a couple of noughts on your fee.

I think of a letter Scott Fitzgerald wrote from Hollywood in 1935 where he was working on the script of *Gone with the Wind*: 'It's nice work if you can get it and you can get it if you try about three years. The point is once you've got in – Screen Credit 1st, a Hit 2nd, and the Academy Award 3rd – you can count on it for ever . . . and know there's one place you'll be fed without being asked to even wash the dishes.'

Later in the day Frears and I drive to West London to check out an actress for the part of Alice. Frears says what a strange cast it is: a mixture of inexperienced young people, a rock singer, a famous and glamorous movie star who's never worked in Britain, and a theatre actress without a great deal of film experience.

The irascible actress we've come to see, in her genteel West London sitting room, starts off by flapping the letter we've written her and saying how flattered she is to be offered the part of Anna. Surely though, at her age, early fifties, she shouldn't be expected to have two Ws tattooed on her buttocks.

I look at Frears. As he sits there in her high-backed leather chair with his ripped green-striped plimsolls resting on her cream carpet, I can't help thinking of him as a punk at heart. He is a little distracted, though perfectly polite. I know what he doesn't like to do is explain things. Art Malik has complained to me that Frears wouldn't explain Sammy's role in the movie to him. Frears said he didn't know that much about Sammy's role in the movie: it's all so much in Hanif's head, he says; let's hope we can pull it out some time near the day. Malik was horrified by Frears's flipness. But Frears wants people to work intuitively and spontaneously. He wants them to work things out for themselves and not be lazy; what they've worked out they'll bring to the film. He also expects other people to be as intelligent as he is.

Frears pulls himself together and hastily explains that the actress is being considered for the part of Alice, not Anna. She then looks at me as if I'm a very small boy and asks, severely, what the film is about. I explain that it concerns a number of relationships unfolding against a background of uprising and social deterioration. 'That's easy to say,' she says. 'Very easy. Now can you tell me what it's about?' I tell her I'm not one of those people who think plays or films ought to be 'about' anything. 'What are you trying to say then?' she asks, putting her head in her hands and making a frightening gurgling noise. At first I think she's choking; I consider hammering her on the back. But surely she's crying? When she looks up I can see she's laughing hysterically. 'Oh, poor England's changed,' she says. 'And I don't know where it's gone. A black boy attacked me in the street the other day. Before, you'd never even lock the door to your house.'

Frears is knocking back a fat slug of whisky and looking in the other direction. The actress starts up on a rambling monologue about her career. She keeps you alert because you have no idea what she's going to say next. In some ways she is rather like Alice, delicate, decent and unable to understand why her world has changed.

16 FEBRUARY 1987
Roland Gift who is playing Danny comes over. He admits being nervous of Frears's method of working, of not rehearsing. I tell him of the dangers of over-preparation which kill spontaneity and creativity; also that he's in the film partly because of what he'll bring of himself to the part, not because of his technical abilities as an actor. The idea is to avoid performances. British actors, because of their training, tend to be theatrical on film.

Roland talks about being brought up in Birmingham and being in a class at school in which there were only five white kids. And then moving to Hull and being the only black kid in the class. The racism was constant and casual. One day he was walking along and heard someone calling out, 'Nigger, nigger, nigger.' When he turned round he saw it was a woman calling her dog.

Later he worked as a nude model for architects. Architects? In a life-drawing class, he says, so the barbarians of the future would get a sense of beauty.

We talk about the character of Danny being underwritten. Roland might fill it out by having a strong sense of what the character is. He thinks there's much of himself he can bring to the part.

Bevan has managed to get permission from the police to block off some streets in North Kensington to stage the riot scenes, or the 'scuffles' as he describes them. They don't even ask to see a script.

17 FEBRUARY 1987
To see Claire Bloom, Stephen and I. Chat for a while to Philip Roth. Roth fizzes and whirls with mischief and vibrant interest in the world. He is a wicked teller of tales! I tell him that on taking his advice and writing some fiction, a story I've written for the *London Review of Books* may not be accepted in the US because of the sex and four-letter words in it. He says he's had similar trouble: imagine the nuisance, he tells me, of having to find a suitable synonym for the perfectly adequate 'dogshit' just so your

story can be published in the prissy *New Yorker*. He also tells us with great glee that he'd written a story called 'The Tormented Cunt', but had to change the title.

Claire looks younger than her fifty-six years and I did want Alice older than that, partly so that the scene I lifted from *A Sentimental Education* – the woman lets down her hair and it has gone white – is effective. Claire hunts through the script for a line she doesn't understand. It is: 'The proletarian and theocratic ideas you theoretically admire grind civilization into dust.' It seems to me that no clearer line has ever been written. Frears explains the line and adds that the line 'that country has been sodomized by religion' in *Laundrette* mystified him long after the film had been finished. Claire looks sceptical and says she doesn't think she can say something she doesn't understand.

On the way home Frears says Shashi has rung to ask if he can leave early on the first day of shooting to go to a cocktail party. Frears says if this is how stars behave, it might all be difficult to deal with.

23 FEBRUARY 1987

I run into Roland. He says: Why does Danny have to have a girlfriend and a kid? I say because it makes the character seem more complex. I can see Roland wants Danny to be more romantic. I tell him the character's unreal enough and idealized as it is.

Talk to Karin Bamborough about the end of the movie. The idea of it ending with the hanging is still not necessarily the best. It'll send people away in a gloomy mood. Karin thinks there should be some image of reconciliation. I say, well, if one occurs to me I'll put it in. I'm not sure Sammy and Rosie should be reconciled at the end of the film, not sure they'd want that.

Stephen and I talk about the music we'll use in the film. Some kind of street music, plus some American soul, perhaps Otis Redding or Sam Cooke, music from the sixties which seems to me to have really lasted, something that everyone recognizes.

24 FEBRUARY 1987

Roland, Ayub and Wendy Gazelle (who has just flown in from New York), are in the production office today and on the walls are photographs of Meera and Suzette Llewellyn, who are playing Rani and Vivia respectively. Ayub and Wendy together look like Romeo and Juliet! Their all being so young will mean there's little bitterness in the film, so a story that involves the shooting of a black woman by the police, an exiled torturer and the eviction of dozens of people from their homes, while ending with a hanging, won't be as grim as this description sounds.

The actors are pretty nervous and complain to me that Frears and I haven't spent much time talking about the backgrounds to their characters. I urge them to work it out for themselves, maybe writing out a few pages of background detail. Despite their worries, when I sit down with them and they discuss various scenes with each other, they seem to know what they're about. The important thing is that they like each other and can relax. I know they've started to hang out together.

Stephen and I talk about the end of the film once more. It's still not worked out properly. Maybe there should be another scene, after the hanging, maybe with Sammy and Rosie in each other's arms, a scene that was cut from earlier in the script. I'm not against the idea; but maybe there's something more interesting I could write.

25 FEBRUARY 1987
To Milan for the opening of *Laundrette* in Italy. I do an interview through an interpreter and go to the bar with the publicist, the distributor and the journalist. They talk politics. The journalist, a fashionably dressed woman in her thirties, turns to me and says: Isn't it funny, all the Italians round the table are communists? It's a disconcerting remark, since I haven't heard anyone describe themselves as a communist for at least ten years, since I was a student. Indeed, I reflect, it's only with embarrassment and in low voices that the people I know in London will admit to being socialists. Generally we don't admit to believing in anything at all, though we sometimes disapprove of the worst abuses. It's as if in London it's considered vulgar or exhibitionist to hold too strongly to anything, hence the London contempt for Mrs Thatcher along with the failure to do anything about her. In some ways this British insouciance is a manifestation of British scepticism and dislike of extremes; in another way it's just feebleness.

To a massive Gothic church in Milan. The stained-glass windows tell, in sequence, like bright cartoons, biblical stories. And with strong sunlight behind each of them, they resemble the frames of a film.

26 FEBRUARY 1987

To Florence by train. The fast and comfortable Italian trains and the businessmen around me in their sharp clothes. The care they take: everything matches; not a garment is worn or shapeless. What surprises me is the affluence and attractiveness of northern Italy and that despite Thatcher's talk about the boom in British industry, compared with this place it's in desperate straits.

In Florence I do more interviews. This publicizing of films is an odd business. I have no Italian money and little grasp of what is going on. Norboto, the publicist, takes me from city to city. When I am thirsty he buys me a Coke; when I am hungry he fetches me a sandwich. He takes me to the hotel and in the morning he wakes me up. It reminds me of being a kid and being out with my father. You veer in these publicity tours between feeling you are important, a minor celebrity, someone to be listened to, and the predominant feeling that you're a kind of large parcel, a property at the disposal of a nervous distributor with which things can be done, films sold and money made. You hope in return that you'll get a decent view of the Grand Canal from the window of your Venice hotel.

27 FEBRUARY 1987

To Venice for the Carnival. I stand in the railway station and read the board: there are trains to Vienna, Trieste, Munich, Paris, Rome. That these places are merely a train ride away gives one a sense of being a part of Europe that isn't available in Britain. When I'm in the US and people talk of making a trip to Europe it still takes me a beat to realize they're also referring to Britain. I think of the legendary sign at Dover: Fog over Channel, Continent cut off.

Then out into the crumbling, drowning city of tourists which is packed with people in medieval costumes and gold masks. They dance all night in St Mark's Square and fall to the ground where they sleep beneath people's feet until morning. Looking at the bridges I wonder how they don't collapse under the weight of people. I walk with the distributor through this wild celebration to a cinema where *Laundrette* is opening. The cinema is virtually empty. A man is asleep and snoring loudly, the sound filling the place. To my horror the film is dubbed: strange Italian voices are coming from the mouths of Saeed Jaffrey and Roshan Seth. The Italian hairdresser on *Sammy and Rosie* said he grew up hearing Cary Grant, Frank Sinatra and Marlon Brando all with the same voice, dubbed by the same Italian actor.

I watch the audience watching the film. At the points where the audience usually laugh there is complete silence. The film is no longer a comedy.

I get up to speak. The snoring man opens his eyes briefly, looks at me and goes back to sleep. The audience puts questions to me through the interpreter. But though she has a good accent, what the interpreter says to me makes no sense. So I describe how the film came to be made and talk a little about the gay theme. She blushes when I say this. Then she stumbles and backs away from me and the microphone. I glare at her. She recovers and talks to the audience for a long time. But I know she isn't repeating what I said. So I turn to her and say the aim of the film is to induce world-wide sexual excitement. Now she won't go to the microphone at all. She is backing away, wide-eyed. The audience whistles and shouts and claps. I get out as soon as I can.

3 MARCH 1987
First day of shooting. I go to pick up Shashi who turned up late last night. 'I nearly didn't come at all,' he says. 'I've got big tax problems. Rajiv Gandhi himself had to sort them out.' Shashi has three Indian writers staying with him in his flat. They're working on a script Shashi will direct at the end of the year. He tells me that Indian film-writers often write ten films a year and earn £250,000. Some writers only work out the story and are no good at dialogue, while others just come in for the verbals.

Shashi looks splendid, if a little plump. He's less familiar with the script than I'd hoped – and in the car he asks me to remind him of the story – but he's serious and keen. Soon everyone is in love with him.

We shoot the scene of Rosie finding the old man dead in the

bath. I turn up and find Frances in a long green coat with a furry black collar. On her head she has a black pillbox hat. Instead of a social worker she looks like an extra from *Doctor Zhivago*. I take it as a direct blow to the heart, as if it's a complete misunderstanding of everything I've been trying to do. Frances is very nervous and apprehensive, as it's the first day, and she clings to the coat as if it's a part of Rosie's soul. But Frears is enjoying himself. He can get along with actors. Where I'd have them by the throat with my foot in the back of their neck, he sits down and talks gently with them. Frances changes the coat. But it's not the last we'll see of that coat.

When Shashi comes on set – we're shooting the scene outside and inside the off-licence – the local Asians come out of their shops in amazement. One immediately gives him three boxes of crisps. Another gives him perfume and aftershave. For them Shashi is a massive star, like Robert Redford, and he has been around for considerably longer, making over 200 films since he first started, aged eight. When they believe it is him, the kids dress up in their best clothes – the Asian girls in smart shalwar kamiz and jewellery – to be photographed with him. Others ring their relatives who come in cars across London and wait patiently in the freezing cold for a break in filming so they can stand next to their idol.

Seeing the off-licence with wire-mesh across the counter, the dogs, the siege-like atmosphere – it is based on places I know in Brixton, where buying a bottle of wine can be like entering a battle zone – Shashi is taken aback, as Rafi would be. Shashi asks: 'Are there really places like this in London?'

Shashi decides to wear a moustache for the part. It makes him look older and less handsome, less of a matinée idol; but also formidable, imposing and sort of British in the right military, authoritarian sort of way.

4 MARCH 1987
Sarah comes to the set where we're shooting a scene between Sammy and Rosie set in a looted Asian grocer's shop. Frances is still tense and unsure and she complains to Frears about Sarah being there watching her as she is trying to create the character of Rosie. Sarah leaves. She is amused by the clothes Frances is

wearing, as if a social worker would wear a mini-skirt and three-inch-high heels to work. Before that, of course, the hours in make-up, the hairdresser constantly standing by to adjust any hair that might fall out of place. All seemingly absurd when the attempt is to do something that is, in some ways, realistic. But then the cinema has never stopped being a palace of dreams. Even in the serious cinema there is some emphasis on the ideal. Imagine casting a film with only ugly or even, just ordinary-looking actors. The cinema cannot replace the novel or autobiography as the precise and serious medium of the age while it is still too intent on charming its audience!

5 MARCH 1987
Much falsity in what I wrote in anger yesterday, partly to do with my failure to let go of the script and let Frears make the film he has to make. I think that despite the clothes and the paraphernalia of glamour, the voice of the film collaborators can transcend the trivial messages of escape that the cinema must transmit if it is to reach a large audience.

Also, and today I have to repeat this to myself, the film-writer always has to give way to the director, who is the controlling intelligence of the film, the invisible tyrant behind everything. The only way for a writer to influence a film is through his relationship with the director. If this is good then the film will be a successful collaboration; if not, the writer has had it. And most writers are lucky if directors even allow them on the set.

Presumably, it is because of this contingency that serious writers don't venture into the cinema. You don't find many American writers – in a country with a film industry – thinking of film as a serious possibility.

Also contra what I said yesterday: I do think the constraints of playing to a wide audience can be useful. You have to ensure that your work is accessible. You can't indulge yourself; you have to be self-critical; you have to say: is this available? So, to take a literary analogy, you have popular Thackeray and Dickens, say, as opposed to some recent American writing, loaded with experiment, innovation and pretty sentences which is published by minor magazines for an audience of acolytes, friends and university libraries.

I wake up, pull the curtains and it is snowing! The snow is settling too. This morning we're shooting the aftermath of the riots, when Rafi decides to go out for a walk. He meets Danny and they go to visit Alice.

When I get to the set the snow doesn't seem to matter. Burntout cars are scattered about; there are mobs throwing rubber bricks and police with batons charging them. Padded stuntmen dive over cars and policemen kick them. Among it all, in the awful cold, wanders Shashi, bearing a bunch of flowers. The kids in the mob are locals, not extras. These kids refuse to sit in the caravan with the actors in police uniform in case their friends think they're fraternizing with the police.

The charges and fighting look terrifying and we haven't shot the main riot yet. That's tonight. Frears says: If we can get through that we'll be OK, we'll survive!

6 MARCH 1987

Night shoot. A row of derelict houses and shops with asbestos over their windows with gas-fired jets in little window boxes in front of them to give the impression of the neighbourhood in flames. In front of this are exploding cars, fire-engines, ambulances and a divided mob of 200 extras plus police with riot shields. There are four cameras. It's massive, for a British film, and brilliantly organized. I think of the script: it just says something like: in the background the riot continues!

The rioting itself is frightening, thrilling and cathartic. It's not difficult to see how compelling and exciting taking part in a riot can be and how far out of yourself such compulsion can take you. On some takes the kids playing rioters continue to attack the extras in uniform after we've cut. Some of the extras playing police threaten to go home if this doesn't stop!

Late at night from the mob emerges a strange sight. Nearby is a hostel for the blind and about fifteen bewildered blind people with dogs emerge from the mob and walk across the riot area as cars explode around them and Molotov cocktails are flung into shops. At the far end of the set they release their dogs into a park.

I see rushes of yesterday's material. It looks pretty effective. I can see how thrilling it must be to film large-scale set-pieces. It's far easier and often more effective than the hard stuff: subtle

96

acting and the delineation of complicated relationships.

Each day Frears asks me to give him a detailed report of the rushes: what was that scene like? he asks. And the other one? He refuses to watch rushes. The discovery that he can avoid this has liberated him from the inevitable discouragement of staring daily at his own work and its limitations.

10 MARCH 1987

More rushes and some of the riot material cut together. At last it comes alive! I talk to Oliver (the lighting cameraman) about the way he's shot it. He's eschewed the pinks and blues of *Laundrette*, going for a more monochrome look, though at times the screen positively glows! Originally I was sceptical of this, liking the heightened and cheap quality of *Laundrette*. But Oliver felt that the more real *Sammy and Rosie* looks the better as the oddness of the story and strangeness of the juxtapositions are sufficient unreality. He has given the film a European quality, sensuous and warm. I haven't seen a film like it made in Britain.

It's a hard film to make and much to do in six weeks. Everyone looks exhausted already, not surprisingly. They start work at eight in the morning and usually knock off around eleven at night. With night shoots we've been starting at six in the evening and finishing at seven in the morning, though people aren't getting to bed till nine.

The worries about Ayub: he's stiff at the moment and the humour of the part is beyond him. He's better in close-up, being handsome. In mid-shot he wilts and looks as if he doesn't quite know what to do with his body. His pleasantness of character comes through, playing against the unpleasantness of Sammy. But it's going to be difficult for him in the first big part he's played. Wendy looks effective in the rushes, powerful and vulnerable. American actors are trained for the screen. Where you sometimes feel Ayub is delivering his performance to the back of the stalls, Wendy understands the intimacy of the cinema.

On the way to today's shoot, in an East End loft, a battleship passes along the river. The taxi I'm in stops. 'Why have you stopped?' I ask. 'I can't go on,' the driver says, gazing at the ship. 'My eyes have misted over. Doesn't it do you in?' I refrain from telling him the battleship is French. When I turn up I find they've managed to work the battleship into the scene. Let's hope people think it's a symbol.

In the script most of the scenes between Anna and Sammy take place in Anna's bed. But Frears opens them up, using the whole space, even creating a new scene by moving into the loft's tiny bathroom which has a spectacular view over London. Because of these scenes I write new dialogue for Anna about an exhibition she's having, called 'Images of a Decaying Europe'.

13 MARCH 1987

Today Frears rails at the actors for lacking flair, for thinking too much about their costumes, for being too passive and not helping him enough. He's been cheerful all through it, but now the strain is starting to tell. It's partly because the scene we're shooting – outside Sammy's and Rosie's flat, with Rosie returning with Danny on a motorbike, the Ghost walking past, Vivia watching Rafi from the window and Rosie's two friends also watching Rafi – is very complicated. The cold – working fifteen hours a day in snow flurries – is getting people down. Frears also blames me for this scene going badly: 'You should never set a scene as complicated as this outside,' he says. 'Haven't you learned that yet? I can't control it out here!' In fact, this is the only scene in the film we will have to reshoot.

16 MARCH 1987

To Frears's last night to discuss the waste ground eviction scene at the end of the film. It has to be choreographed precisely and it hasn't been yet. What I've written isn't clear. So we work out, almost shot by shot, the final relationships between the characters. The problem with the end of the film, with the eviction as opposed to the already shot riot scene, is the danger of it being sentimental. Ambiguities and ironies have to be excavated just as Rafi and Sammy and Anna bumbling around during the riots made all the difference to a scene which could easily be one-dimensional.

Have the idea that in order to reflect on what has gone on in the film it might be a good notion to have, during the closing credits, some of Anna's photographs shown to us.

Shooting the waste-ground material on the large piece of unused ground under the motorway. Bit of a shock to turn up at the location and find Frances Barber in a black and white corset. I look at her wondering if she has forgotten to put the rest of her clothes on. Her breasts, well, they are jammed into an odd shape: it looks as though she has two Cornish pasties attached to her chest. I tell Stephen she looks like a gangster's moll from a western. He takes it as a compliment. 'That's exactly what I intended,' he says. 'John Ford would be proud of me.'

Between takes, the corset debate continues between us, as in a snowstorm Shashi sits in a filthy flea-ridden armchair in front of a smoking fire, surrounded by young people in grey costumes banging tins. Frears argues that the corset is an inspired idea; it liberates Rosie from do-goodery; she looks bizarre, anarchistic and interesting, not earnest or condescending. What he then describes as the 'simplistic politics of the film' he says are transcended by imaginativeness. At the end of the argument he calls me a prude and for the rest of the afternoon he refers to me as Mrs Grundy.

The corset depresses me because after everyone's work on the film it is still easy to hit a wrong note. I feel uneasy in complaining because I think Frears's judgement is less conservative than my own; I could be wrong. Maybe, too, I'm being sentimental about the woman the character is based on, a more dignified and sensitive person than the one signified by the corset.

19 MARCH 1987

We shoot the eviction and exodus from the waste ground. With the trailers and caravans whirling in the mud and dust, the bulldozers crashing through shops, lifting cars and tossing them about, the straggly kids waving flags and playing music as the police and heavies invade and evict them, it is like a western! Frears runs among it all, yelling instructions through a megaphone.

It is tough on Shashi. India's premier actor, a god to millions, is impersonating a torturer having a nightmare while bouncing on a bed in the back of a caravan which is being wildly driven around a stony waste ground in a snowstorm. Books scatter over his head.

When he emerges, shaken and stirred, dizzy and fed up, he threatens to go back to Bombay. The next morning, when we tell him as a joke that we have to reshoot his scene in the back of the caravan, he goes white.

It is obvious that he has a difficult part. The character of Rafi is complex and contradictory and he has to play against many different kinds of character. Shashi is not used to making films in English and the part is physically demanding. But with his modesty, generosity and unEnglish liking for women, he is the most adored person on the film.

So a glorious day – mostly to do with the pleasure of working with other people, especially the 'straggly kids' who jam all day and some of the night by the fire. Most of them are alternative comedians and buskers from the London Underground. Few of them have a regular place to live, and when Debbie wants to inform them of a day's shooting, she has to send her assistants round the tube stations of central London to find them.

Coming out of my hutch for this film has made me realize how hard it is sometimes to bear the isolation that all writers have to put up with.

20 MARCH 1987
To Kew where we're shooting the suburban material – in Alice's house and the street she lives in. We film the scene where Alice comes to the door and sees Rafi for the first time for thirty years. We do several takes and find it works best when Claire and Shashi do least, when they contain their reaction and we have to strain to imagine their feelings.

Here, where it is quiet and sedate, leafy and affluent, we have more complaints from residents than at any other location, though there are no charging bulldozers and we burn nothing down, though severely tempted.

Being brought up in the suburbs myself, this location reminds me of slow childhood Sundays on which you weren't allowed to yell in the street and your friends were kept in for the holy day. Sundays in the suburbs were a funeral and it's still beyond me why the celebration of God's love for the world has to be such a miserable business.

I know now that England is primarily a suburban country and

100

English values are suburban values. The best of that is kindness and mild-temperedness, politeness and privacy, and some rather resentful tolerance. The suburbs are also a mix of people. In my small street lived a civil servant, an interior decorator, secretaries, a local journalist, an architect, a van driver, a milkman, and so on, all living together in comfortable houses with gardens, in relative harmony.

At worst there is narrowness of outlook and fear of the different. There is cruelty by privacy and indifference. There is great lower-middle-class snobbery, contempt for the working class and envy of the middle class. And there is a refusal to admit to humanity beyond the family, beyond the household walls and garden fence. Each family as an autonomous, self-sufficient unit faces a hostile world of other self-contained families. This neurotic and materialistic privacy, the keystone of British suburban life, ensures that the 'collective' or even the 'public' will mean little to these people. It's interesting that the Labour leader, Neil Kinnock, has repudiated the now discredited notion of the collective in favour of left-wing individualism. He has said: 'They have got to be told that socialism is the answer for them because socialism looks after the individual.'

My love and fascination for inner London endures. Here there is fluidity and possibilities are unlimited. Here it is possible to avoid your enemies; here everything is available. In the suburbs everything changes slowly. Heraclitus said: 'You can't step in the same river twice.' In the inner-city you can barely step in the same street twice, so rapid is human and environmental change.

I sit in the first sunshine of the year in this English garden in Kew reading the papers. There is much written today about the verdict in the Blakelock case, where a policeman was hacked to death during an uprising on the Broadwater Farm Estate in North London. A man was sentenced to life imprisonment for the killing. The uprising followed the death of a much respected middle-aged black woman, Cynthia Jarrett, who died of a heart attack during a police raid on her home on the estate. The Police Commissioner, Sir Kenneth Newman, claimed that 'anarchists and Trotskyists' planned the uprising in advance, though there is no evidence for this. There is confusion and inconsistency in the police account of the incident, to say the least. The police also broke numerous rules and acted illegally in their treatment of two young 'suspects'. A fifteen-year-old boy was held three days without access to his parents or a solicitor. A sixteen-year-old, with a mental age of seven, was interrogated without his mother or solicitor.

It's all depressing, as was the incident around which I based the opening of the film: the shooting of a black woman, Cherry Groce, who was permanently paralysed after being shot during a police raid in which her son was being sought.

But what are we doing using this material in the film? Today, when confronted once more by the racism, violence, alienation and waste of the Broadwater Farm Estate uprising, our little film has to be justified over again. After all, real life has become part of a film, reduced perhaps, maybe trivialized. We will make money from it; careers will be furthered; film festivals attended. But aren't we stealing other people's lives, their hard experience, for our own purposes? The relation we bear to those people's lives is tangential, to say the least. Perhaps because of that we seriously misunderstand their lives.

I can't work out today if the question about the relation between the real people, the real events, and the portrayal is an aesthetic or moral one. In other words, if the acting is good, if the film is well made, if it seems authentic, does that make it all right, is the stealing justified? Will the issue be settled if experience is successfully distilled into art?

Or is the quality of the work irrelevant to the social issue, which is that of middle-class people (albeit dissenting middle-class people) who own and control and have access to the media and to money, using minority and working-class material to entertain other middle-class people? Frequently during the making of the film I feel that this is the case, that what we're doing is a kind of social voyeurism.

At the same time I can justify our work by saying it is the duty of contemporary films to show contemporary life. This portrayal of our world as it is is valuable in itself, and part of the climate of opposition and dissent.

In one part of me I do believe there is some anger in the film; and it does deal with things not often touched on in British films. In another part of me, when I look at the film world, run by the usual white middle-class public-school types, with a few parvenu thugs thrown in, I can see that the film is just a commercial product.

Frears and I talk this over. He says the film is optimistic about the young people portrayed in it: their vivacity, lack of conformity and rebelliousness are celebrated in it.

20 MARCH 1987

In the evening to rushes – uncut takes of the waste-ground material. It looks good and people are pleased with their work. Leon from Cinecom is there, as is his boss. Leon sleeps through the rushes and his boss says: For rushes they're not bad, but it's not family entertainment.

After, we drive through London and go to a pub. It's a shock that London and other people's lives are continuing while we're making a film. Film-making is an absorbing and complete world; the relationships are so intense and generous, the collaboration so total, that the rest of the world is blanked out.

24 MARCH 1987

In the studio at Twickenham at last and off the street. Here we're shooting all the material in Sammy's and Rosie's flat. It is easier to watch the performances in this calmer and more controlled place, even if the atmosphere is slightly flat.

It seems to me that Shashi is going to turn out to be very good, portraying a complex and dangerous character, a murderer and a man eager to be loved, a populist and an élitist. Frears is carefully and patiently teasing out the power and subtlety in Shashi by getting him to act simply and underplay everything. You can see the performance developing take by take. After eight or nine takes Shashi is settled, a little tired and bored, more casual and relaxed. Now he is able to throw the scene away. And this is when he is at his best, though he himself prefers the first few takes when he considers himself to be really 'acting'. Sometimes he can't see why Frears wants to do so many retakes.

Ayub improving too. He is inexperienced as an actor (it is of course difficult for Asian actors to gain experience), but Oliver is doing a wonderful job in making him look like a matinée idol. The balance of the script has gone against Sammy. It is Rafi and

Rosie that I've developed as there is more scope for conflict with them. Sammy doesn't believe in a great deal, so it's hard to have him disagree much with anyone. His confusion isn't particularly interesting. Rosie is a more complex character and harder to write, especially as she isn't a character I've written before.

25 MARCH 1987

I turn up on the set and find that Frears has Rosie going out to meet her lover not only in that ridiculous coat, but wearing only her underwear. He seems to think that someone would go to see their lover, via a riot, wearing only a thermal vest and a pair of tights. I certainly wouldn't. I hope I'll be able to watch the film in the future without suffering at this moment.

Thank God I'm leaving London in a couple of days for the Oscar ceremonies. I've been on the set every day, though I'm not sure it's been as essential as it was on *Laundrette*. There hasn't been much rewriting this time.

28 MARCH 1987

Los Angeles. I wind down the window of the cab as we hit the freeway and accelerate. Air rushes in, gloriously warm to me after an English winter of freezing balls. I pull three layers of clothes over my head. LA is blazingly green and bright: how easy it is to forget (one's senses accustomed to dullness) that this industry town is also subtropical; its serious and conservative business takes place among palm trees, exotic birds and preternaturally singing flowers. Everything is as resplendent as if I'd taken LSD. Walking into the hotel, the Château Marmont, a small, friendly European place on a hill, the grass appears to have been sprayed with gloss and the air pumped full of perfume. It is eucalyptus.

The phone calls begin as soon as I open the windows of my room: from agents, press people, producers, recommending the numerous totally beautiful human beings I should impress in the next few days. I say to my agent: But most of these people do not interest me. She says: Dear, all that is important is that you interest them – whatever you do, don't discourage them. As long as they're saying your name as they eat all round this city you've got nothing to worry about.

As we talk I eat some fruit. Swollen nature in my hands:

strawberries long as courgettes, thick as cucumbers. Here the most natural things look unnatural, which is fitting in a mythical city in a hotel in which Bogart proposed to Bacall, where John Belushi died, where Dorothy Parker had an apartment and Lillian Hellman and Norman Mailer would come to tea and no one wanted to be the first to leave, and in which, when I get into bed to read – Robert Stone's *Children of Light* – I find myself staring into a novel about a burned-out screenwriter living at the Château Marmont drinking and drugging himself while a screenplay he wrote is being shot in another country.

29 MARCH 1987
At breakfast the waiters are discussing films they've seen recently. Then they start to worry about the Oscars. They can't believe that *Betty Blue* is the French entry in the Best Foreign Picture Category. What about *Vagabonde*? At another table a young man is hungrily explaining the plot of a film he's written to an older man. 'This film could change lives,' he says, not eating. The other man eats croissants as big as boomerangs. 'It's about an alien disguised as a policeman. But it's a good alien, right? It's about the renewal of the human spirit.'

Later, with some friends, I drive through this baking city to Venice Beach. I'm being shown the city. How attractive it is too, and not vulgar. I notice how few black people there are. What little poverty. I'd have thought this city was bereft of unhappiness if I hadn't stayed downtown on my last visit here. That time the manager of the hotel said, when I checked in: Whatever you do, sir, don't go out after dark.

Venice Beach – so called because of the rotting bits of Venetian architecture still left over from a time when a minor Venice was being contemplated here. It is in its wild spirit something like the Venice, Italy, I saw a few weeks ago, though less stylish and more eccentric, which you'd expect in a country without an aristocratic culture. Herds of people cruise the boardwalk. A man is juggling a chainsaw and a ball, hurling the humming saw into the air and catching it. A dog in sunglasses watches. A man with pierced nipples, with rings hanging from them, also watches. All along the beach there are masseurs, rolfers, shiatsu experts, astrologers, yoga masters and tattoo freaks. Further along, at Muscle Beach, in an enclosed area, men and women work out, twitching, shaking, vibrating, tensing and generally exhibiting their bodies to the crowds.

Back at the hotel the phone rings constantly. People tell me: The greatest day of your life is approaching. I try to think of the one day in my life in which I had more happiness than any other.

Later, to a cocktail party given by Orion, the distributors of *Laundrette* in the US. It is as interesting as a convention of carpet salesmen. I sit next to a woman whose husband is an executive in the company. In her early twenties, she tells me how she hates it all, how you just have to keep smiling if you want your husband to be promoted and how desperate she is to go home and get some drugs up her nose. Everyone leaves early. Drive the LA streets at eleven and they're deserted. It's like Canterbury. Everyone goes to bed early because they work so hard.

30 MARCH 1987

After lunch in Santa Monica near the beach, to the Bel-Air hotel with its lush gardens, its white Moorish architecture and its private suites and cottages in the grounds with their own patios. Here, you go somewhere, get out of your car and someone parks it. When you leave the restaurant, bar or hotel, the car is waiting outside. If you've got the dough, there's always someone around to save you doing something yourself. I'm beginning to see how addictive such a luxurious place as this could become. Once you'd really got the taste for it, how could you be detoxicated? To which clinic could you go to dry out from the juices of wealth and pleasure that had saturated you in this city?

It's interesting how few notable American film directors actually live in Los Angeles: Coppola, Pakula, Pollack, Scorsese, Demmie, all live in other cities. The directors and writers who do live here are British, often successful in British television, now flailing around in the vacuum of Los Angeles, rich but rootless and confused, attempting the impossible task of finding decent work, exiled from a country that doesn't have a film industry.

31 MARCH 1987

The day of the Oscars. People leave work after lunch in order to get home and watch it on TV at five o'clock. All over the city

Oscar parties are beginning in lounges and beside pools. For weeks since the nominations, there has been speculation about possible winners. Turn on the TV and grave pundits are weighing the merits of Bob Hoskins and Paul Newman; open a paper and predictions are being made. Here the Oscars are unavoidable, as competitive and popular as a Cup Final, as dignified and socially important as a Royal Wedding.

A last swim on my back in the hotel pool, watching the sky through the trees before the extensive pleasures of the bathroom where I sip champagne and receive phone calls and gifts. Slipping on my elastic bow-tie I suspect this will be the best time of the day. Outside in the lane the limo is already waiting. By now I have definitely had enough of people saying: It's enough to be nominated, it's an honour in itself. By now that isn't enough: by now I want to win; by now, I know I will win!

When your four-seater black stretch limo pulls up outside the venue all you see on either side of you are other limos, a shimmering sea of shining black metal. When you slide out, you see the high grandstands lining the long walk to the entrance. In these packed grandstands screaming people wave placards with the names of their favourite films written on them. '*Platoon, Platoon, Platoon!*' someone is yelling. Another person bellows: '*Room with a View, Room with a View!*' One man holds a placard which says: 'Read the Bible.'

Inside there are scores of young people, the women in long dresses, the men in tuxedos, who have small signs around their neck saying: 'The 59th Academy Awards'. They are the seat-fillers. Their role is essential, so that when the cameras sweep across the auditorium there isn't an empty seat in the place, whereas in fact the sensible people are in the bar watching it all, like everyone else, on TV, only going in to sit down for their bit. In the bar with friends we look out for stars and discuss them: doesn't Elizabeth Taylor look tiny and doesn't her head look big – perhaps she's had all the fat in her body sucked out by the modish vacuum method; doesn't Bette Davis look shrivelled and fragile; doesn't Sigourney Weaver look terrific and what was wrong with Jane Fonda and doesn't Dustin Hoffman always look the same?

When it comes to your section and Shirley MacLaine starts to read out the names of the nominees, you silently run over your speech, remove a speck of dried semen from your collar and squeeze the arms of your seat, ready to propel yourself into the sight of a billion people. You wonder where in the sitting room you'll put your Oscar, or maybe you should hide it somewhere in case it's stolen? What does it weigh anyway? You'll soon find out.

When they make a mistake and don't read out your name you vow never to attend any such ridiculous ceremony of self-congratulation, exhibitionism and vulgarity again.

1 APRIL 1987
The next day by the pool drinking iced tea, several young producers come by. My impression is that they come to have a look at you, to check you out, to see if there's anything in you for them. One drives me around the city in his Jag. He asks me if I want to fly to San Francisco for lunch. I ask if there isn't anywhere a little nearer we can go. He swears eternal love and a contract.

An idea for a story: of someone who inadvertently writes a successful film and lives off its reputation for years, so afraid of ending the shower of financial seductions and blandishments that he never writes anything again.

2 APRIL 1987
I return to find Frears in heaven on the set, sitting with his plimsolls up and gossiping, waiting for a shot to be set up. To ruin his day I tell him about the directors I've met in Hollywood and how much they earn and the kind of luxury in which they live. Frears goes into agonies of frustration and jealousy, especially when I mention money. He keeps saying: 'What am I doing here, fuck all this art, just give me the money!' This makes Shashi laugh and laugh. But there is another element of neurosis in all this American craziness which is more serious, especially for a film-maker. Since the 1950s the United States is the place where the action is, where things happen, and because the US has the central role in the world which England had in the nineteenth century, America is always present for players in the culture game. Like a mountain that you have to climb or turn away from in disgust, it is an existential challenge involving complicated choices and threats and fear. Do you make an attempt on this height or do you withdraw into your corner? How much of

yourself are you prepared to put into this enterprise? Unfortunately for British film-makers, America has been something of a Bermuda Triangle into which many careers have crashed without trace.

They are shooting the party scenes and some kissing between Rani and Vivia; also between Rani and another woman, Margy. I remember Meera (who plays Rani) as a student coming to see me in 1981 at Riverside Studios where we were rehearsing a play for the Royal Court. She asked me if I thought she would ever become an actress. She desperately wanted to go into the theatre, and she wanted to write too. There was some resistance from her parents who, like the parents of many Asian girls, were mostly concerned with her having an arranged marriage. But her enthusiasm and ambition were so obvious, I just told her to stick at it. I wonder what her parents would say if they could see her having a grape removed from between her teeth by the tongue of another actress!

Perhaps these kisses, like the ones between Johnny and Omar in *Laundrette* –

Each kiss a heart-quake, – for a kiss's strength
I think it must be reckon'd by its length.

– are subversive in some way. It's as if they poke social convention and say: There are these other ways to live; there are people who are different, but aren't guilt-ridden. When I went to see *She's Gotta Have It* recently, and it was mostly a young black audience, when the two women kissed the audience screamed with disapproval and repulsion.

We also shoot the scene where Rafi arrives at Sammy's and Rosie's flat and finds Rosie's friends putting a condom on a carrot. Later in the scene Rani and Vivia stand in the centre of the room and kiss, rather ostentatiously. Shashi is agitated by all this and yells for his agent, a taxi, and a first-class flight to Bombay.

God knows what this film will look like when it's all stuck together. I suppose it's a film of juxtapositions and contrasts, of different scenes banging hard together. One danger is that the film lacks narrative force and focus; it may be too diffuse.

3 APRIL 1987

Frears and I rejig the scene where Rafi comes home from the

party and finds Vivia and Rani in bed. Originally they chase him around the room with lumps of wood and attempt to beat him to a pulp. He barricades himself in the study and climbs out of the window and down the drainpipe. When it comes to shooting it, it doesn't seem as believable or funny as when I wrote it.

So at lunch-time we rework it. Rafi comes in, finds Vivia and Rani in bed, and is outraged. Abusing them in Punjabi, a row breaks out. So Shashi and Meera work out a couple of pages of abuse to scream at each other. Meera will also throw things at him. It's terrifying when we come to shoot it, with Meera hammering a piece of wood with nails in it into the door behind which Shashi is cowering! As the scene is all Punjabi abuse we talk about putting sub-titles on it.

7 APRIL 1987

We shoot Sammy and Rosie crying and rocking together on the floor at the end of the film, with the women slowly leaving the flat behind them. I get to the studio at eight in the morning and leave at nine in the evening. This seems to me to be an ideal solution to living: erect this saving girder of necessity around you: you don't have to think or decide how to live!

Frears saw a good deal of the film on Saturday, as it's being edited as we shoot it. He says: Christ, it's a weepie, a complete heartbreaker! We'll have to put hundreds of violins on the soundtrack!

8 APRIL 1987

I look at a good chunk of the film on the tiny screen of an editing machine at Twickenham Studios. It makes me laugh, partly, I think in relief that it isn't completely terrible. It's less rough than *Laundrette*, more glamorous, more conventional, with Hollywood colours. I look at the scene where Rafi catches Rani and Vivia in bed; they attack him and he climbs out of the window and down the drainpipe. We were thinking of cutting him climbing out of the window, it seemed unconvincing. Yet looking at it in context, I think it'll work.

Frears comes into the cutting room while I'm watching and talks to Mick, the editor. It's very impressive the way Frears can hold every shot of the film in his head at once, even though he's barely seen any of it. He can remember every take of every shot. So when he's talking to Mick about scenes he shot weeks ago, he'll say: Wasn't take 5 better than take 3? Or: Didn't the actress have her hand over her face on take 11 on the mid-shot and not on take 2?

We talk about the kind of harmless threat of disorder that films like *Laundrette* or *Prick Up Your Ears* represent, which partly explains their success. The pattern is one of there being a fairly rigid social order which is set up in detail in the film. Set against this order there is an individual or two, preferably in love, who violate this conventional structure. Their rebellion, their form of transgressional sex, is liberating, exciting. Audiences identify with it. Films as diverse as, say, *Billy Liar*, *Room with a View*, *Midnight Cowboy*, *Guess Who's Coming to Dinner?*, have this pattern, following an alienated individual or couple, unable to find a place for themselves in the society as it is. Usually there's some kind of individual reconciliation at the end of the film; or the individual is destroyed. But there is rarely any sense that the society could or should be changed. The pattern is, of course, a seductive one because we can see ourselves in the alienated, but authentic, individual standing up against stuffiness, ignorance and hatred of love. In all this we are not helped to think in any wider sense of the way societies repress legitimate ideals, groups of people, and possible forms of life.

In some films of the middle and late sixties, when the rigid social order was eschewed entirely as no longer relevant, and only 'liberated' individuals were portrayed, the films have little power or interest, lacking the kind of conflict and tension that the classic pattern necessarily produces.

9 APRIL 1987
Filming in the cellar of a pub in Kew. Cramped and dusty; the lights keep going out. Claire, whose performance until now has been, rightly, contained, starts to reveal her power in this cellar scene with Shashi. Furiously jerking things out of the suitcase she packed thirty years ago, and shoving the whole lot on the floor, she reveals such a combination of wild anger, vulnerability and pain, that when the camera cut, there was complete silence. Even Shashi looked shaken. It was especially difficult for her as the Ghost was in the scene as well, standing at her elbow.

We spend the day in a South Kensington restaurant filming the confrontation scene between Rosie, Rafi and Sammy when they go out to dinner. This is the pivotal scene of the movie. It starts off simply. The three of them are at the table; the violinists play a little Mozart in the background, the drag queen sits behind them. But the violinists have extraordinary faces: English features, pale shoulders (ready to be painted by Ingres), Pre-Raphaelite hair, and after twelve solid hours of fiddling, very worn fingers.

As the day progresses Shashi and Frances become more heated in their argument. The playing of the violinists becomes more frenzied. The drag queen does a very exasperated flounce. Shashi eats a finger made from sausage meat and spits out the nail, putting it politely on the side of the plate.

I can see Frears's imagination racing as he uses these few elements to their fullest and most absurd effect. He becomes increasingly inventive, his control and experience allowing him to play. I am a little afraid the scene will be drowned in effects, but I did write the scene in a similar spirit – putting the people in the restaurant and experimenting until something came of it.

Of course, the conditions of Frears's creativity are different from mine. Alone in a room I can take my time and rewrite as often as I like. I can leave the scene and rewrite it in two weeks' time. For Frears in that small restaurant crowded with seventy people there is no way of going back on the scene. It has to be done there and then and it has to work. It takes a lot of nerve to play with a scene under those conditions, especially as the medium is so ridiculously expensive.

I notice how comfortable Frances is in her part now. She has discovered who she is playing; and that is something you find out only in the course of filming. But unlike the theatre, there's never another opportunity to integrate later discoveries into earlier scenes.

If the conditions in which film directors usually work make it difficult for them to be original, a film actor's life is certainly no bed of roses. You are picked up at seven or earlier in the morning; you may shoot your first scene at ten or eleven, if you're lucky. Or you may be hanging around until three or four before you begin work. Wendy came in early for several days, thinking they were going to shoot her 'fuck night' scene with Ayub that day, then nothing was done, though she didn't know that until early evening. But if your scene is going to be shot, however bored and cold and confused by the entire thing you are, you have to drag your concentration to the sticking place, you have to pull out your performance immediately. You may have to play a very emotional scene and you have to play it now! But whatever you're doing, it's very expensive, so the faster you do it the more you will be appreciated. As there's little time for exploration and experiment you will probably have to give a performance much like one you've given before because at least you can be sure it will work.

When that acting job's finished there might possibly be another one. Should you turn it down and hope something better will turn up? Perhaps it won't; but perhaps it will. If it does, the director may be duff or the script no good or the part too small. Whatever happens, most of the work actors get doesn't stretch them and 80 per cent of the directors they work with will have little talent. Of the good 20 per cent, 5 per cent will be tyrants who think of actors as puppets.

Despite these difficulties, all the British actors I know have one thing in common: they are well-trained, skilled and dedicated people who want to do good work and give of their best within a profession that only rarely gives them the opportunity to reach their potential. No wonder so many actors become neurotic or dull through lack of interest in anything but their careers.

11 APRIL 1987
In a tiny studio off the Harrow Road we film the interior scenes set in Danny's caravan. Outside the caravan, a row of gas jets reproduce the waste ground fires. The props man and the assistant art director wearily dance behind the gas jets to reproduce the celebration of the 'fuck' night as Frances and Roland roll around naked. Frears sinks down in a chair next to me. 'I've become completely paranoid,' he says. 'I've had it. Is this any good or not?' 'I don't know,' I say. 'What's it about anyway?' he says. 'Fuck knows,' I reply. He needs support and for no one to speak in too loud a voice. Anything above a whisper is interpreted as hatred. 'We should have had more time,' he says, after a while. 'About two more weeks would have done it. But it would have

cost £300,000 and we didn't have it.'

I leave early and go to a book publishing party. On the way I see the police have stopped a black man and woman and are questioning them. It's odd going to the party: the world going on as normal. Later, I see someone I recognize coming towards me, black hair sticking up, face white, a week's growth on his face. I try and work out who it is. At last I know: Stephen Frears.

Later, I run into a friend who drags me away from the restaurant and tells me to sit in her car. She says there's something I have to see that I've never seen before. Well, she drives me to an Arts Centre in West London. I take one look at the scene and try to leave. It looks as if she's brought me to an Asian wedding. Women and kids of all ages are sitting on rows of chairs around the walls, not talking. The men, mostly Sikhs, stand together at the bar, talking. The women have gone to a lot of trouble tonight, really dressing up for this one in much jewellery, in shalwar kamiz's threaded with silver and gold. By ten o'clock the hall is packed with Asian families, with babies and children and old men and women. I've no idea what to expect. The stage is full of rock 'n' roll gear.

The band comes on: eight men in red and white costumes. They look like assistants in a fast-food joint. One of them announces the singers: 'Welcome the greatest Bhangra singers in the world!' Two men bounce on stage in spangled T-shirts and tight white pants.

The music starts. The music is extraordinary. After years of colonialism and immigration and Asian life in Britain; after years of black American and reggae music in Britain comes this weird fusion. A cocktail of blues and r 'n' b shaken with Indian film songs in Hindi, cut with heavy guitar solos and electric violin runs and African drumming, a result of all the music in the world being available in an affluent Asian area, Southall, near Heathrow Airport – it is Bhangra music! Detroit and Delhi, in London!

For a few seconds no one moves. The dance floor is a forbidden zone with everyone perched like tense runners around it. Then no one can hold themselves back. Men fly on to the floor. They dance together, thrusting their arms into the air and jerking their hips and thighs, tight-buttocked. Sometimes the men climb on each others' shoulders or wrap their legs around the others' waists to be swept in dizzy circles inches from the floor. Women and girls dance with each other; women dance with tiny babies. An old Indian colonel with a fine moustache and military importance weaves amongst it all, taking photographs.

And they all know each other, these people. They were at school together and now they live in the same streets and do business with each other and marry amongst themselves. This gig, such a celebration, is unlike any other I've been to for years: it's not to do with boys and girls trying to pick each other up; it's not aggressive. Makes you aware of the violence and hostility you expect of public occasions in Britain.

Now we've almost finished filming, in the morning I sit down and try to write something new.

I've enjoyed being out of the house every day and the intense involvement of film-making. The cliché of film-making which talks of the set as being a family is inaccurate, though the set is hierarchical and strictly stratified in the family way. But unlike with a family the relationships are finite, everyone knows what they're doing and there's a strong sense of purpose. The particular pleasure of a film set is in being with group of people who work well and happily together.

Now, back at the desk, I immediately feel that writing is something of a dingy business. Why this unhealthy attempt to catch life, to trap it, rearrange it, pass it on, when it should be lived and forgotten? Why this re-creation in isolation of something that had blood and real life in it? The writer's pretence and self-flattery that what is written is even realer than the real when it's nothing of the kind.

16 APRIL 1987
To Frears's house. He's being photographed with his kids to coincide with the opening of *Prick Up Your Ears*. David Byrne comes by in a green and black tartan jacket, jeans, with a little pigtail. He has a luminous round face, and bright clear skin. It's the first time I've met him, though his band, the Talking Heads, are heroes of mine. We walk round the corner to the Gate Diner where the waiter inadvertently sits us under a poster for *Stop Making Sense*. Various people in the street recognize him and a woman comes over to our table and gives him a note with her

phone number on it, thanking him for his contribution to music and films.

Byrne is shy and clever and unpretentious. The disconcerting thing about him is that he listens to what you say and thinks it over before replying seriously. The only other person I've met who has done this is Peter Brook. A most unusual experience.

Byrne was given the script of *Sammy and Rosie* in New York by the great fixer David Gothard, and wants to do some music for it. Byrne has picked up some African music in Paris, composed by street musicians, which Frears thinks is superb. Byrne talks about using similar rhythms in the music he might do for *Sammy and Rosie*. We'll show Byrne a cut of the movie as soon as possible and he can put music over the parts that interest him. The problem is time, as Byrne is composing the music for the new Bertolucci film, *The Last Emperor*, as well as writing the songs for the new Talking Heads record.

In the street waiting for a cab with Byrne I see the cops have stopped another car with black people in it. The black people are being very patient. What the hell is going on in this city?

18 APRIL 1987
Big day. First rough assembly of the film. I meet the editor, Mick Audsley, who is pulling the film on a trolley in its numerous silver cans through the streets. It's 110 minutes long, he says. As it's a rough-cut the film is a little like a home movie, with the sound coming and going; and of course there's no music.

We watch it in a small viewing theatre off Tottenham Court Road. The first forty minutes are encouraging and absorbing and we laugh a lot. Shashi is excellent: both menacing and comic, though his performance seems to lack subtlety. I am elated all the same. Then it begins to fall apart. My mind wanders. I can't follow the story. Entire scenes, which seemed good in themselves at the time of shooting, pass without registering. They bear no relation to each other. It is the centre of the film I'm referring to: the party, the 'fuck' night, the morning after, the breakfasts. Towards the end the film picks up again and is rather moving.

Each of us, cameraman, editor, director, me, can see the faults of the thing from our own point of view. I can see the character of Danny fading out; can see that the character of Anna is not

116

sufficiently rounded; that the riots are not developed in any significant way.

But there are pluses: Shashi of course. And Frances, who portrays a strong, complex person very clearly. Roland too, especially as I'd worried that he might have been a little wooden.

What I don't get is any sense of the freshness of the thing, of how surprising and interesting it may be to others.

After, I stagger from the viewing theatre, pleased on the one hand that it's up on the screen at last. On the other, I feel disappointed that after all the work, the effort, the thought, it's all over so quickly and just a movie.

Frears is pleased. These things are usually hell, he says, but this wasn't, entirely. Some of it, he says, is the best work he's done; it's a subtle and demanding film. Part of the problem with it, he thinks, is that maybe it's too funny at the beginning and not serious enough. He suggests it could be slowed down a bit. I say I don't want to lose any of the humour especially as the end of the film is so miserable. It's a question, over the next few weeks, of reconciling the two things.

30 APRIL 1987
Mick Audsley has been furiously cutting the film for the last two weeks. When we all walk into the preview theatre – including Karin Bamborough and David Rose from Channel 4 – to see how the film's progressed, Mick's as nervous as a playwright on a first night. I reassure him. But it's his film now; this is his draft; it's his work we're judging. 'I've taken some stuff out,' he says nervously. 'And moved other things around.'

There are about twelve people in the room. Frears's film *Prick Up Your Ears* is successful in the States and Bevan's *Personal Services* is number three in the British film charts, so they're both pretty cheerful.

For the first forty minutes I can't understand what's happened to the film. It's more shaped now, but less bizarre somehow, less unpredictable. I suppress my own laughter in order to register every gurgle and snort of pleasure around me. But there is nothing: complete silence.

The film begins to improve around the 'fuck' night and takes off when the Ghetto-lites dance and mime to Otis Redding's 'My

Girl' and we cut between the avid fuckers. It's unashamedly erotic, a turn-on, running right up against the mean monogamous spirit of our age. There must be more jiggling tongues in this film than in any other ever made.

I cringe throughout at the ridiculousness of the dialogue, which seems nothing like the way people actually talk. A lot of this will go, I expect, or we can play some very loud David Byrne music over it, though I am attached to some of the ideas contained in the more strident speeches.

At the end I feel drained and disappointed. I look around for a chair in the corner into which I can quietly disappear. I feel like putting a jacket over my head.

Then you have to ask people what they think. David Rose is a little enigmatic. He says the film is like a dream, so heightened and unreal it is. It bears no relation to the real world. I say: We want to create a self-sustaining, internally coherent world. He says, yes, you've done that, but you can't be surprised when what you've done seems like an intrusion to those it is about.

Frears says it's a different film from the one we watched two weeks ago. Now we have to fuse the seriousness of this version with the frivolity of the first version.

A journalist who came to see me the other day asked why I always write about such low types, about people without values or morality, as it seems all the characters are, except for Alice. It's a shock when he says this. I write about the world around me, the people I know, and myself. Perhaps I've been hanging out with the wrong crowd. Reminds me of a story about Proust, who when correcting the proofs of *Remembrance of Things Past*, was suddenly disgusted by the horrible people he'd brought to life, corrupt and unpleasant and lustful all of them and not a figure of integrity anywhere in it.

4 MAY 1987
A very confused time for us in trying to work out what kind of film we want to release. We talk frequently about the shape of it, of pressing it experimentally all over to locate the bones beneath the rolling fat. But you have to press in far to touch hardness. There's barely any story to the thing. If there is a story, it belongs to Shashi. Frears is talking of 'taking things out', he says, 'Less

means better' and adds ominously, 'There's far too much in it.' It's painful, this necessary process of cutting. I think, for consolation, of Jessica Mitford's: 'In writing you must always kill your dearest darlings!'

7 MAY 1987
Frears on good form in the cutting room. He hasn't been so cheerful for days. He's cutting swathes out of the movie. It's funnier and more delicate, he says. He adds: Your talent will seem considerably greater after I've done with it!

He's put his finger on something which will inevitably bother film-writers. If the movie is successful you can never be sure to what extent this is due to you, or whether the acting, editing and direction have concealed weaknesses and otherwise lifted an ordinary script which, if it were to be shown in its entirety or as written, wouldn't work at all.

11 MAY 1987
Frears rings and says it's vital I come in later today and see the film. You'll have to brace yourself, he adds, ringing off.

The first shock is in the first minute: the shooting. Mick has obviously worried a great deal about this. He has removed the moment when the black woman gets shot, when you see her covered in blood and falling to the ground. Even Frears is surprised that this has come out, but he's pleased with it. What such a powerful and upsetting moment does, they both argue, is overwhelm the opening. Frears also says that its removal improves the subtlety of the story-telling – we find out later what has happened. I do like the shooting, not for aesthetic reasons, but for didactic ones: it says, this is what happens to some black people in Britain – they get shot up by the police.

Halfway through this cut I can see it's going to work. The shape is better, it's quicker, less portentous. Danny's long speech has gone, as have various other bits of dialogue. A scene between Anna and Sammy has gone, which means that Anna's part in the film is diminished. Alice's speech on going down the stairs, before the cellar scene, has gone, which I missed. I'll try and get them to put it back.

I argue to Frears that in some ways the film has been

119

depoliticized, or that private emotions now have primacy over public acts or moral positions. In one sense, with a film this is inevitable: it is the characters and their lives one is interested in. Frears argues that, on the contrary, the film is more political. Ideas are being banged together harder now: the audience is being provoked. But I can see that my remark has bothered him.

I can't deny it's a better film: less grim, less confused and lumpy, funnier and maybe tearjerking at the end. Frears has put the music from *Jules et Jim* over the scene where Sammy tells us what he likes about London, which brings that section to life, thank God, especially as three or four people have moaned about it being redundant. Next week Frears will shoot a couple more sections for that particular homage to Woody Allen and maybe reprise the music at the end.

After the viewing we talk about there being another scene at the very end of the film, a scene between Sammy and Rosie under a tree, maybe at Hammersmith, by the river. Of course, there's the danger of sentimentalizing this, of saying that despite everything – the shooting, the revolts, the politics of Rafi – this odd couple end up being happy together, the implication being that this is all that matters. This is, of course, the pattern of classical narration: an original set-up is disrupted but is restored at the end. Thus the audience doesn't leave the cinema thinking that life is completely hopeless. I say to Frears that at least at the end of *Jules et Jim* Jeanne Moreau drives herself and her lover off a bridge. He says, sensibly: Well, let's shoot the scene and if it doesn't work we can dump it.

17 MAY 1987
Frears and I talk about the odd way in which *Sammy and Rosie* has developed. The oddness is in not being able to say in advance what kind of film it is since the process seems to have been to shoot a lot of material and then decide later, after chucking bits of it away, what the film will be like. It's like a structured improvisation. Frears says: Shouldn't we be more in control at the beginning? Surely, if we had more idea of what we're doing we could spend more time on the bits we're going to use? But, with some exceptions, it's difficult to tell what's going

to be in the final film, partly because I'm no good at plots, at working out precisely what the story is.

21 MAY 1987

Frears and I were both moaning to each other about the Tory Election broadcast that went out yesterday. Its hideous nationalism and neo-fascism, its talk of 'imported foreign ideologies like socialism' and its base appeals to xenophobia. Seeing the film once again Frears has taken the socialist Holst's theme from 'Jupiter' in *The Planets*, later used for the patriotic hymn 'I Vow to Thee my Country' (which was, incidentally, played at the Royal Wedding) from the Tory broadcast, and played it over the eviction scene, giving it a ritualistic quality.

Later there is intense discussion of the film between David and Karin, Mick, Bevan, Frears and I. I find these discussions quite painful. But Frears invites them. He listens carefully to everything people have to say and then he goes back to the film. So secure is he in what he is doing that he isn't threatened by criticism; he can absorb it and use it to improve his work.

An Election has been called. I do some leafleting for the Labour Party. I cover estates which I walk past every day, but haven't been inside since the last Election. In the meantime, the buildings have been 'refurbished'. From the outside the blocks and low-rise houses look modern: rainproof, wind resistant, nature-blocking. I wonder if they have really changed since the last time around. My trips to New York and Los Angeles now seem utterly unimportant when there are parts of my own city, my own streets, for Chrissakes, five minutes walk from me, that are unknown to me!

I walk off the main road and across the grass to the entrance of the first block. The door is open; the glass in the door is smashed. A woman in filthy clothes, in rags I suppose, stands in the entrance waving her arms around. She is in another place: stoned. I go on through and into the silver steel cage of the lift. Inside I hold my nose. At the top of the block the windows are smashed and the wind blows sharply across the landing. Broken bottles, cans and general detritus are whisked about.

Someone has a sign on their door: 'Don't burgle me I have nothin'.' Many of the doors have been smashed in and are held together with old bits of wood. The stench of piss and shit fills the place.

An old distressed woman in a nightdress comes out of her flat and complains that a party has been going on downstairs for two days. One man comes to the door with a barely controlled Alsatian. Come and take back this fucking leaflet, he screams at me; come and get it, mate!

There are at least two dogs on each floor, and you can hear their barking echo through the building.

It is difficult to explain to the people who live here why they should vote Labour; it is difficult to explain to them why they should vote for anyone at all.

23 MAY 1987
Last day of shooting. Bits and pieces. Colin McCabe at the ICA, Sammy and Rosie by the river (for the last shot of the film) and Aloo Baloo at the Finborough pub in Earls Court for the 'Sammy and Rosie in London' part of the film. It is a strange day because these are all things Sarah and I have done together; they are places we go. So you live them and then go back a few weeks later with some mates, a camera, and some actors, and put it all in a film. Sarah has yet to see the film and that's good, I think, as it is improving all the time. But she rang me last night, angry at being excluded, thinking this was deliberate, or just more evidence of my general indifference. Whatever it is, she has started to call the film 'Hanif Gets Paid, Sarah Gets Exploited'.

5 JUNE 1987
Frears and Stanley Myers are working away on the music. Charlie Gillett, the great rock DJ and music expert, is suggesting various bands and styles of music to go over different parts of the film. David Byrne, from whom we've heard not a word for ages, has finally said he's too busy to do anything.

Sarah finally comes to see the film. She sits in front of Frances Barber. After, she tells me she likes it. She confidently says she can see it as an entire object, just a good film, something quite apart from herself.

10 JUNE 1987
My agent Sheila goes to see the uncompleted *Sammy and Rosie* and rings this morning. Some of it's wonderful, she says. But it's

heartless and anti-women. Why anti-women? I ask. Because all the women in the film are shown as manipulative. And Rosie doesn't care for Sammy at all. When he sleeps with someone else it doesn't appear to bother her. I thought, she says, that this was because you were going to show Rosie as a lesbian. I ask her why she should think this. Because most of her friends are lesbian. Plus, she adds, you make Sammy into such a weak, physically unattractive and horrible character it's difficult to see how she could take much interest in him. Is he what you and Stephen think women like?

Sheila doesn't like the end of the film, with Sammy and Rosie sitting crying on the floor. It makes them seem callous, especially with all the women trailing out of the flat and not doing or saying anything. In addition she dislikes the 'Sammy and Rosie in London' sequence, one of my favourites in the film, which she compares to a cheap advertisement. That just has to go, she says, it's so ridiculous. Anyway, couldn't at least fifteen minutes of the film be cut? Like what? Well, Alice's speech to Rafi on walking down the stairs, just before the cellar scene. One doesn't listen to all this, she says. Well, I feel like saying, we could chop fifteen minutes out. But that would make the film just over an hour long. We'd have to release it as a short.

For a while after this conversation I am perforated by doubt and think Sheila might be right; our judgement has gone and the entire thing is some terrible, arrogant mistake.

There's going to be at least another eighteen months of this, of exposure, of being judged. This is a 'profession of opinion' as Valéry calls it, where to make a film or write a book is to stand up so that people can fire bullets at you.

I go off to the dubbing theatre where the actor playing the property developer is yelling into the mike about communist, lesbian moaning minnies. This will be put through a megaphone and added to the eviction scene. Frears is in good cheer as ever. When I tell him about Sheila's attack on the film he says we will get attacked this time around. People will want to engage with the issues the film raises; they'll want to argue with the movie and they'll get angry. It won't be an easy ride as with *Laundrette* or *Prick*, with people just being grateful these kinds of films are being made at all.

As we walk through Soho, Frears and Mick are talking once more about the shooting of the black woman at the beginning of the film. They're now thinking of putting it back. It's a hard decision to make: do you forfeit an important and powerful scene because it throws out the balance of the film?

I spend the evening leafleting the estates again, as it's the day before the Election. The feeling in the committee room, where people are squatting on the floor addressing envelopes, is that it'll be close. No one actually thinks we'll put an end to Thatcherism this time, but at least Thatcher won't have put an end to socialism.

I'd seen Kinnock at a Labour rally held in a sports hall in Leicester on Friday. There are at least 2000 people there and it is strictly an all-ticket affair: they are very nervous of hecklers, as the meeting is being televised. There is a squad of large women bouncers who, when a heckler starts up, grab the dissident by the hair and shove her or him out of the hall at high speed. They are also nervous of anything too radical: I've been instructed not to use the word 'comrade' in my speech, though it is Kinnock's first word.

The Labour organization has wound up the crowd expertly and they are delirious, kicking out a tremendous din with their heels against the back of the wooden benches. When I introduce Kinnock, he and Glenys come through the hall surrounded by a brass band, pushing through photographers and fans like a couple of movie stars.

Kinnock speaks brilliantly, contrasting levity and passion, blasting off with a string of anti-Tory jokes. I know that various sympathetic writers and comedians have been sending lines and gags round to his house and he's been working them into the speeches he always insists on writing himself. The impression is of someone who is half stand-up comic and half revivalist preacher. What is also clear is his humanity and goodness, his real concern for the many inequalities of our society. At the end of the meeting the crowd sings 'We Shall Overcome' and 'The Red Flag' and we cheer and cheer. For these two hours I can't see how we can fail to win the Election.

15 JUNE 1987
Everyone reeling from the shock of the Election defeat and from

the knowledge that we were completely wrong about the extent of the Labour failure. We lost in Fulham by 6000 votes, though we'd won the seat at a recent by-election. Someone tells me that the people on the estate I leafleted voted 3 to 1 for the Tories. What this Tory victory means is the death of the dream of the sixties, which was that our society would become more adjusted to the needs of all the people who live in it; that it would become more compassionate, more liberal, more tolerant, less intent on excluding various groups from the domain of the human; that the Health Service, education, and the spectrum of social services would be more valued and that through them our society would become fairer, less unequal, less harshly competitive; and that the lives of the marginalized and excluded would not continue to be wasted. But for the third time running, the British people have shown that this is precisely what they don't want.

We invite a bunch of friends to a showing of *Sammy and Rosie*, mainly to look at two significant changes: one is the putting back of the shooting of the black woman; the other the inclusion of Roland's long speech about domestic colonialism.

Well, as we stand around in the preview theatre, some people argue that we don't need the shooting as it's too obvious. Others say you need its power and clarity. I can see that Frears has made up his mind in favour of it at last. I can also see that he is glad to have put back Roland's speech as it anchors the first half of the film and gives Danny's character more substance. The hardest scene to decide about is the very end, with Sammy and Rosie walking by the river. Frears says he hates unhappy endings, so he'd added it to lighten the tone. But someone else says it gives the movie two endings; and, worse than that, it's an attempt to have it both ways – to cheer up what is a sad and rather despairing film.

Despite these bits and pieces, I feel it now has shape and thrust and pace, due to the incredible amount of work Frears and Mick Audsley have done in the editing.

Sarah also comes to this screening, and we leave together, walking down Charing Cross Road. She has said little so far and when I ask about the film this time around, her reaction is more ambiguous. She says: 'Yes, this time it wasn't so easy. Rosie seemed too hard and uncaring; surely I am not hard and uncaring? Perhaps I am like that and haven't been able to see that side of myself?

Perhaps that is your objective view of me. Oh, it's difficult for me because I have had the sensation recently, when I'm at work or with a friend – it just comes over me – that I'm turning into the character you've written and Stephen has directed and the actress has portrayed. What have you done?'

19 JUNE 1987

Frears exceedingly cheerful and enjoying finishing the film, putting the frills on, playing around with it. He never stops working on it or worrying about it. He talks about using some of Thatcher's speeches: over the beginning, he says, just after the credits, the St Francis speech would do nicely. And somewhere else. Where? I ask. You'll have to wait and see, he replies.

Stanley Myers, who is in charge of the music, gives me a tape of music which has been put together by Charlie Gillett. It's terrific stuff: bits of African rhythms, reggae, and some salsa and rap stuff.

8 JULY 1987

To see the almost finished *Sammy and Rosie*. It's been dubbed now; the sound is good and the music is on. Frears has put back the scene between Anna and Sammy where she pushes him half out of her studio and interrogates him about his other girlfriends. I thought this scene had gone for good, but Frears continues to experiment. He'd said it would be a surprise where he'd use the Thatcher material. It is. It's right at the front, before the credits, over a shot of the waste ground after the eviction. It works as a kind of prologue and hums with threat and anticipation, though with its mention of the 'inner city' it also seems to be presenting an issue film. But anger and despair following the Election have gone straight into the film, giving it a hard political edge. Frears's struggle over the last few weeks has been to reconcile those two difficult things: the love of Sammy and Rosie for each other, and the numerous issues that surround them. At last he's given the story a clarity and definition I couldn't find for it in the script.

I sit through the film in a kind of haze, unable to enjoy or understand it. I can see how complete it is now, but I have no idea of what it will mean for other people, what an audience seeing it freshly will make of it. Only then will the circle be complete. We'll just have to wait and see.

After the screening someone says how surprised they are that such a film got made at all, that somehow the police didn't come round to your house and say: This kind of thing isn't allowed! Of course it won't be when the new Obscenity Bill goes through.

Later that night I go out for a drink with a friend in Notting Hill. We go to a pub. It's a dingy place, with a dwarf barmaid. It's mostly black men there, playing pool. And some white girls, not talking much, looking tired and unhealthy. On the walls are warnings against the selling of drugs on the premises. Loud music, a DJ, a little dancing. A fight breaks out in the next bar. Immediately the pub is invaded by police. They drag the fighters outside and throw them into a van. People gather round. It's a hot night. And soon the air is full of police sirens. Six police vans show up. The cops jump out and grab anyone standing near by. They are very truculent and jumpy, though no one is especially aggressive towards them. We leave and drive along the All Saints Road, an area known for its drug dealers. Twice we're stopped and questioned: Where are we going, why are we in the area, what are our names? Black people in cars are pulled out and searched. Eventually we park the car and walk around. The area is swamped with police. They're in couples, stationed every twenty-five yards from each other. There's barely anyone else in the street.

14 JULY 1987
A showing of *Sammy and Rosie* at nine in the morning. Frears and Audsley have been working all weekend, juggling with bits and pieces. It seems complete, except for some music which has been put on over the cellar scene and seems to dissipate the power of Claire's performance at that point. Otherwise the film works powerfully, with a lot of soul and kick. We talk about how much has gone back in and Frears says how foolish it seems in retrospect to have taken out so much and then put it back. But of course that process of testing was essential, a way of finding out what was necessary to the film and what not.

We stand outside the cutting room in Wardour Street and Frears says: Well, that's it then, that's finished, we've made the best film we can. I won't see it again, he adds, or maybe I'll run it again in five years or something. Let's just hope people like it.